THE
UNEXPECTED
COMMUNITY

The

Unexpected

Community

Portrait of an Old Age Subculture

Arlie Russell Hochschild

UNIVERSITY OF CALIFORNIA PRESS
Berkeley, Los Angeles, London

University of California Press
Berkeley and Los Angeles, California
University of California Press, Ltd.
London, England

Printed in the United States of America

1 2 3 4 5 6 7 8 9

For Adam, David and Gabriel

CONTENTS

PREFACE

The Contradiction of Aging in America

One out of ten people in the United States is over sixty-five. According to the U.S. Census Bureau projections, this proportion could rise to as high as 19 percent by the year 2025. Then it will be relevant to more people to ask: What makes some healthy old people socially alive and others, equally healthy, withdrawn and disinterested in the world? We can turn, for one clue, to the immediate social context—the potential friends that live, or don't live, next door. Something that might at first seem a superficial matter, a mere question of where one lives, can in some cases have a surprisingly deep effect on the shape and feel of the old person's social world.*

Work and family are for most middle aged Americans the main spheres from which social bonds grow. But for the old, ties to work and in some ways to family are attenuated, if not completely cut off, causing many to be isolated and feel lonely. Social isolation, as it has become "normal" for America's old, is not humanly inevitable, for the very trends in family and work life which make isolation a problem in the first place are not inevitable.

Old age communities around the country, like the one described here, are for the most part a good *response* to these problematic trends, but *not* a fundamental *solution* to the problems these trends incur. Old age communities can help alleviate unwanted isolation. But they still face another, more systematic, pervasive and implacable problem: the old are forced to relinquish their economic function, while at the same time, *as a stratum* they are socially denigrated for no longer being economically useful, for being outside the market economy—society's dependents. There is nothing inevitable about the relation we assign between age and retirement, nor between retirement and uselessness, nor between uselessness and unworthiness. Nor do all societies burden their old with this chain of associations. When we compare our society with preindustrial societies and with what we might forecast for postindustrial society,** we see the differing "fit" between

* For a more detailed exposition of these factors, and a critique of one of the principal theories of aging, disengagement theory, see my "Disengagement Theory: A Critique and Proposal" (*American Sociological Review* 40 (October 1975): 553–569.

Originally this was a case study to disprove the theory of disengagement, or rather, to show that old people disengage under certain social conditions but not under others. Impressive empirical evidence for this already comes from Irving Rosow's *The Social Integration of the Aged*. In that work, as Chapter 2 points out, Rosow shows that old people who live among other old people make more friends than old people who live among young people. This book shows why and how this happens. For the original study see "A Community of Grandmothers," Ph.D. Dissertation, University of California, Berkeley, 1969.
** The three models vary in the degree of similarity between the status

what the economy in each case allows the old, and what prevailing social values reward.

In preindustrial societies, a large proportion of old people owned or controlled the mode of production—their land, tools, craft implements. As they grew older, they could thus more easily determine whether to continue to work and maintain the social ties that go with work. The family, as yet undifferentiated from the sphere of work, offered access to work. In addition, there were social rewards for "keeping one's boots on," for extending the social and economic aspects of middle age as long as one could. Consequently there was a *congruence* between what the economy allowed and what social values rewarded. An old person could and usually did continue to work as much as was physically feasible. And this was publically approved.

Ironically, in postindustrial society an entirely different form of *congruence* between what the economy allows and what social values reward is likely to prevail. Given the continued expansion of large corporations, and the decline of small enterprises, it is likely that very few people will control or own the mode of production. The decision of whether or not to work past age 65 will no longer be a "private" one. Each individual's decision will have to take into account the *company's* system of benefits, the *company's* financial incentives to retire at 55, 60, 65, or 70. Most important, the market economy will have developed so far, and production will have become so efficient and mechanized that many people of all ages will be unemployed throughout their lives. Future social values may gradually render nonproductive roles acceptable. There could thus be a congruence between what the economy allows the old person and what the values will reward.

---

of the young and the old. In both the pre- and postindustrial models, the young and old have similar relations to work, but for different reasons. In the preindustrial societies, both young and old do work with use value; the old are not thrown off the market, for they were never in it. In postindustrial societies, both young and old form a large and culturally accepted sector of the non-working population, supported by an expanded welfare system. It is only in the industrial model that the old are devalued *relative* to the young, for economic reasons.

Old people will not work but will feel useful and honored nonetheless.

In contrast, in our present industrial society there is a painful *incongruence* between what the economy offers the old person and what the social values reward. Our economy does not encourage work for people past the age of 65, and yet in subtle ways, old and young alike tend to denigrate the nonworker in general. Status based on what one "has done," like status based on "how one was born" is thinly based compared to status based on "what one is doing," and "what one will do and be." Even now that plans that call for mandatory retirement at 65 have been judged illegal, old people are still subject to financial incentive systems that make it profitable for them to retire early.* These incentive systems are not within their personal control, for they do not own or control, or have a vote in, the large organizations that determine these policies. Most people are forced out of the market economy into activities with use value—care for the home, hobbies, volunteer work.

Here is the rub; the old are judged, and judge themselves, against the standards set by those who work. Like housewives, the old find themselves in a society in which money determines value. Yet they, as a group, remain outside the money economy. Their doings are not worth money, and therefore "not worth anything."** It is possible to have a society in which unpaid activities are genuinely honored, because they are useful. For example, old people in the People's Republic of China retire (men at 60, women at 50) to do work with "use value"—the rearing of children

* In 1977 Congress agreed to amend the Age Discrimination and Employment Act of 1967. This Act had established legal protection against discriminatory employment practices for people of ages 40 through 64. The new legislation moves that upper age limit to 70. This establishes the older person's legal *right* to work. However, the trend in the U.S., as well as in Europe, is toward early retirement. In 1974, Social Security found that 72 percent of its new recipients were *under* age 65. In Europe, polls show that a majority favor leaving the labor force before 65, provided income remains adequate.
** See Margaret Benston, "The Political Economy of Women's Liberation," in *Women in a Man-made World*, eds. Nona Glazer-Malbin and Helen Yougelson Waehrer (Chicago: Rand McNally, 1977).

under three, the teaching of children about the "bitter past," participation on neighborhood committees. The old in China appear to be genuinely respected in large part for these reasons. One can also imagine a society in which unuseful (i.e., recreational) activities are not discredited for people in general and for the old in particular.

But it is precisely in a society such as ours, with a value system which honors what is systematically withheld from old people, that the status of the old declines precipitously.

The community that I describe in this book does not insulate its members against this fundamental contradiction. Their social world expresses and reflects this contradiction (see Chapter 6). As what Hannah Arendt has called "workers without work," their leisure has a work-like caste. The comradely social bonds of their past work in the shipyards, at the lunch counter and in the laundry have become, in part, a model for social bonds in retirement.

Just as these old people are workers without work, they also value the family while they themselves do not live in the midst of one. Family relations, too, become a partial model for the social relations in leisure life. One finds, as I shall show, a horizontal sibling bond, rivalrous, based on similarity, with occasionally, too, self-elected mother hens tending child surrogates. Thus, the social world of the residents weaves together aspects of the comradeship of the shipyards, and the bonds of large families. Drawn from among the least privileged members of society, caught in this contradiction of a society in transition, they have constructed from the resources available to them, one solution to the problem of feeling useless and isolated. This is their story.

About This Book

This book is for several kinds of readers. It is first of all for those with a personal interest in old age—their own, their parents', or other people's—and for those concerned with old age as a social problem. Second, it is addressed to social scientists interested in subcultures and age stratification, and, third, to doctors, social workers, and others who give care to old people. I hope housing officials read the book, too, since I would like to persuade them to build more of the kind of low-income housing for the old described here.

Notes designated by asterisks are for all readers and are at the bottom of their respective pages. Numbered footnotes are addressed to social scientists[1] and are at the back of the book.

Throughout the book, I refer to people over 65 as "old" people. It is a commentary on our culture that I should have felt (but mostly resisted) the impulse to soften the term to something like "older people," or "elderly" people, or even "senior citizens," an unfortunate phrase suggesting a large boy scout with a gold watch. Many minority groups with good reason become sensitive to the titles applied to them, and so it is in this case. There is no word to denote people over 65 that has the exact connotations I would like. I prefer the term "old" because it is straightforward and it sets the tone of this book apart from others that ride over an urgent social problem by saying, in effect, "old age can be rewarding *after all.*"

This book is mainly about a group of forty-three old people who lived in a small apartment building near the shore of San Francisco Bay. However, many of the things I found there reflect on other old people in the United States as well. One reason I have written this book is that these forty-three people were not isolated and not lonely. They were part of a community I did not expect to find. Ironically, these conservative, fundamentalist widows from Oklahoma and Texas and other parts of the Midwest and Southwest are among those least likely to talk about "communal living" and "alternatives to the nuclear family" even while they have improvised something of the sort.

The book tells about their community as a mutual aid society, as a source of jobs, as an audience, as a pool of models for growing old, as a sanctuary and as a subculture with its own customs, gossip, and humor. It tells about friendships and rivalries within the community as well as relations with daughters, store clerks, nurses, and purse snatchers outside. It goes into a good deal of homely detail about such things as the insides of people's living rooms, their refrigerators and photo albums, what they watch on television, whom they visit, and what they think of other old people. Throughout the book theoretical speculation pops up from the data in a not altogether systematic way. But in each case I have sought to show what the community does for and means to the people in it. Altogether, I hope this book suggests an alternative both to the quietly devastating isolation of old age, and to the private and individual solutions to what is a public and collective problem.

Acknowledgments

Sorokin's essay, "Amnesia and New Columbuses" warns those who lack the humility to think they have a new idea or two. One's debt to all the old Columbuses in sociology goes without saying but Georg Simmel and Erving Goffman have been especially important for me.

I would like to give warm thanks to the residents of Merrill Court senior citizen housing project; to Professor Neil Smelser, who has been supportive and helpful; and my thanks to Professors Robert Blauner, Irving Rosow, Alan Wilson and Harold Wilensky for thoughtful comments on an earlier draft. For other kinds of help, my thanks to Scott Belford, Gladys Blankenship, Pat Jordan Fabrizio, Janice Steinberg, and from Prentice-Hall, Ed Stanford and Helen Harris. Thanks also to Will Mangas for his fine copyediting.

I should also mention some other kinds of debts: to the late Leonard Libbey, my grandfather, who shared with me his journalist's eye on the social life of St. Petersburg, Florida, to Mrs. Arlie Libbey, to the late Len Libbey Jr. and to Ruth Russell who made useful comments on an earlier draft, and to Francis Russell who, among many other things, corrected the proofs.

I owe most of all to my husband, Adam, about whom I find it hard to say anything. I will simply mention his warm, continual encouragement and the time he has taken from his work to wage a quiet campaign against "sociologese." I take whatever credit or blame for this book is left.

chapter one

A SOCIOLOGIST'S DIARY

Having all holidays, I am as though I had none . . . Each day used to be individually felt by me . . . I had my Wednesday feelings, my Saturday night's sensations . . . I can spare to go to church now, without grudging the huge cantle which it used to seem to cut out of the holiday. Had I a little son, I would christen him, NOTHING TO DO, he should do nothing.

Charles Lamb
An Essay of *Elia*

Mon.	10:00	Service Club Meeting
	12:00	Pot luck Lunch
	1:00	Workshop on Church Bazaar
	4:00	Tin Class
Tues.	10:00	Workshop
	1:00	Bowling League
	3:00	Visit Pine Manor Nursing Home
	4:00	Christmas Party Comm. Meeting
Wed.	10:00	Workshop
	1:00	Social Service Comm. Meeting
	2:00	Birthday Committee
	7:00	Bible Class
Thurs.	10:00	Workshop
	11:00	Bake Sale, Shopping Plaza
	4:00	Bingo
Fri.	10:00	Workshop
	12:00	Pot luck Lunch
	2:00	Band Practice
	5:30	Open Supper

Weekly Schedule
Merrill Court

Normally, in books such as this, what the author finds and how he or she finds it are reported separately. This separation gives the findings themselves a certain aseptic quality, while the impurities of doing research are neatly packaged under an uninviting chapter title such as "methodology." The reader, in turning the page from the methodology section to Chapter One, assumes a certain faith in Chapter One that he may have lacked the page before. Please consider this chapter as an integral part of the rest, and the methodology as part of the "findings." The chapter deals with how I got into the subject and how I researched it. It then describes the old people themselves and their setting.

I got into the study of old age by accident. My original interest[3] in the community life of the working class had taken me to a white blue-collar suburb on one fringe of San Francisco Bay. One sunny Saturday afternoon, as I walked slowly up and down the tidy rows of small, squat homes topped with TV aerials, I saw few adults, children, or even dogs outside. Apart from the high school area there was no street life such as one finds in city ghettos. What community life there was centered in the tiny bars wedged between auto shops and secondhand stores on the main commercial streets, and in the bowling alleys. A lot of people had gone out to fish in what remains of a rural preserve to the north. I visited the city hall and talked to the Recreation and Parks Director, who was working on Saturday, and he told me of an available job as assistant recreation director in a "senior citizen" housing project. I took it, thinking I might learn something of the history of the community from those who had lived in it.

The residents were fairly easy to get to know. There were forty-three, including thirty-five widows, three couples, and two single men. Since the majority of widows set the social tone of the place, I will sometimes refer to all of the residents as widows, although not all of them were. As I grew to know them, it became clear that the most important thing about the residents, to them and to me, was not their social class, nor the nebulous community at large, but the fact that they were all roughly the same age and lived in a vibrant community of old people.

Thus, I entered Merrill Court* in 1966 to work for three summers and parts of three years, initially not as a sociologist but as an assistant recreation director. When a few months later I told the residents that I was also a sociologist doing a study, it did not seem to bother them. Quite a few were pleased at the idea, but to most it did not seem to mean very much.

One reason why most survey studies in the field of aging do not deal with lower-class old people is that, as two authors rightly noted, "Lower class people are difficult to communicate with and require special interviewing techniques," [2] The residents would be highly suspicious of a sociologist who asked permission to question them for three or six hours and then disappeared. One of the first things I learned was that it was considered impolite to "pry." They do not ask one *another* many questions. Rather, they seem to volunteer answers to silent questions. Question-asking may be a habit more common to professionals who meet many people superficially than it is to those who know a few intimately. The very idea of a one-shot set of questions assumes something about the customs that govern acquaintanceships, and the ways one makes up for the lack of a shared past. To the residents it seemed unnatural. They seemed to be telling me with their friendly silence, "You'll find out about us if you stick around."

This does not mean that I asked no questions. My official role in the community was as a "reporter" for the *Merrill Court Gazette,* a monthly newsletter of events and biographies that I began to edit when I first started working. Part of my job as reporter was to collect biographies and to report them in the monthly newsletter. Part of the biographical material, the cheery part, went into the *Gazette,* and part of it went into my files. The widows enjoyed telling their life histories and were usually

---

* The places and people in this study are real; the names are not.

plain about what they wanted made public and what kept private. This is a book about their public life together and what they cared to keep private is not in print. A woman would come to me as the "chronicler" of the group to add something to her biography, or someone else's, or to fill me in on "the goin's on" of the Merrill Court Service Club. After the first three months I was regularly called by three informal assistant reporters and occasionally by four or five others. With their help, I gradually built up fairly complete files on all but six of the residents.* Most of the time, however, I did not ask questions, or even talk much. I watched, joined in the work, and did errands for the Recreation Director** and the Service Club president.

I should say what the apartment building itself looked like, since the way it was built allowed certain social patterns to emerge that might not have otherwise. It had five floors: a ground floor with one apartment and a large Recreation Room for common use, and four other floors with ten apartments on each floor. There was an elevator midway between the apartments, and a long porch extended the length of all the apartments. It was nearly impossible to walk from any apartment to the elevator without being watched from the series of living-room windows that looked out onto the porch. This was because the chairs inside each living room were arranged so as to face the window and the television at the same time. A woman who was sewing or watching television in her apartment could easily glance up through the window and see or wave to a passer-by. Those in the apartments closest to the elevator saw the most passers-by

---

* I learned about these six indirectly from their neighbors. One of the six was seldom there because she often visited her daughter. Three were in poor health and didn't feel up to talking with an outsider. One had an unreliable memory and others in the building thought him "a bit off, poor thing." He reported eight occupations in my first interview—including doctor, lawyer, lumberjack, and circus entertainer. The last was a religious woman who would reply to my questions with quotes from the Bible; she was generally known as a "religious fanatic."
** She was a half-time city employee.

and were the "informants" about the whereabouts of people on their floor. It seems to me that I saw more people by simply sitting in the "television chair" than I ever did knocking on doors.

Initially, my watching went on in the Recreation Room, where I sat and did handiwork at a table with five or six others. As I drove residents to the doctor, to the housing office, to church, and occasionally to funerals, joined them on visits to relatives, shopped with them, kept bowling scores, visited their apartments and took them to mine, I gradually came to know and like them. Through sharing their lives I came to see how others treated them and how their own behavior changed as their audience did. Finally, I lived at Merrill Court for two weeks, sleeping in a sleeping bag under a bird cage as a guest of one of the widows.

Most of my goals concerning Merrill Court coincided with most of theirs. However, as a person of a different age and social class, and as a sociologist, my perspective differed from theirs. I thought the widows were old and they did not think they were. I thought that, as welfare recipients, they were poor; they thought they were "average." I initially felt that there was something sad about old people living together and that this was a social problem. They did not feel a bit sad about living together as old people, and although they felt that they *had* problems, they did not think that they *were* one.

The meanings they attached to gestures and words were not always the same as mine. For instance, one woman told me in the first biographical interview that she "didn't neighbor much." When I lived with her for two weeks, three years later, she daily received about six visits from neighbors and friends and reported this as typical. What she initially meant by "neighboring" was *having meals* with a neighbor; to her, borrowing a piece of butter or bread, asking for a telephone number, or coming to talk over a television program did not count.

Much of my work[3] involved bringing my definition of the situation closer to theirs or being clear about just how the two differed. It also involved comparing my observations and interpretations with those of other studies of old people, and this led me to wonder to what extent differences in findings are due to differences in methodology. For example, national surveys show that old people find themselves alone over half of the time and the same holds true for the residents at Merrill Court. However, during my visits in their apartments, the residents received roughly one telephone call an hour. The monthly phone bill of one widow recorded 413 message units, not including phone calls received. If two widows are each physically alone in their apartments, on each end of a phone call, are either of them "alone"?

Again, research on lower-class old people shows that only a small proportion read much, know about national public issues or vote; and generally, the Merrill Court residents also fit this description. However, as I discovered, they were very well informed about issues and events that *they* thought important. Although most of the residents were typical of other working-class samples in that they did not know the names of the school board candidates or who was Secretary of State, they were likely to know the name of a photography shop where they bought a school ring for a grandchild, the price of yarn at five nearby stores, and the birthdays of some twenty or thirty grandchildren and great-grandchildren. It is not that these studies automatically assumed that working-class old people knew altogether less than middle-class old people. Rather, what they *did* know much about was simply not recorded in these studies.

It is true that the resident mentioned above did not "neighbor much," that American old people are physically alone half of the time, and that they are unlikely to know the names of local officials. But the more I got to know the residents, the more I saw that information such as this is part of a young middle-class picture of lower-class, old people.

The Residents and Other Old People

The residents of Merrill Court are not a collection of individuals, but a community. Collectively they have devised a solution to one of the most crucial problems of old age—loneliness. In this section I will describe the residents with two questions in mind: Is such a community available to *any* older person who finds himself in a similar social context, or is the social life here due to the characteristics of these particular residents? How typical are they of old people in the United States today?

On one hand, the community members have lived a unique version of their generation's social history, and I will describe it since it suggests what experience they have brought to their present communal enterprise. On the other hand, the *general* outline of their lives is not so very different from that of other Americans of their age, as the comparison with the nation's old people will show.

Most were born on farms or in small towns in the Midwest and South, the daughters of farm hands, migrant workers, lumberjacks, and mill workers. Most were third generation in this country and could carry the family chronicle that far. For example, Daisy recalled:

> My great-granddaddy, Jerry Jenks, was a homesteader. He forded the Mississippi River in covered wagons. He planted the first stake in Clark County, Iowa . . . came from Columbus, Ohio to start with. He was the first judge and the first settler in Clark County. . . . I remember stories they told me of my great-granddaddy making ammunition in the evenings to use against the Indians.

Others came from more humble origins. As Irma recounted:

> Daddy was a dirt farmer, raised in Mississippi. His daddy gave him a span of mules at 24. We had cotton and vegetables, horses and cows. I lived in a log house 'til I was four. There was bigger farms around but we had a nice span of mules and a good set of tools.

Another, the daughter of a migrant worker, did not know her father. "I remember my mother, makin' the shuck mattresses we slept on. She had a hard time. All nine of us got the Asian flu and typhoid fever when it went 'round." The grandfather of another resident came West with the gold rush and stayed to farm. "He had a hard time when he first came out. Ever read Steinbeck's *Grapes of Wrath?* There ain't a lie in that book." *

Most were born quite literally on the farm—in the farmhouse and not in a hospital. Birth, like death, happened at home and as children nearly all of them had hovered near, but had been barred from witnessing, these primal events. They averaged seven brothers and sisters, although many siblings were lost to typhoid epidemics, and had long since been quietly buried in the backyard. From the biographies one gets a picture of a mother taxed by many children, setting her young toddlers to work early. As Daisy proudly noted about her childhood on an Iowa farm: "I had to get up on a chair to do the dishes. That's how early I started workin'." As they grew older, they were assigned more tasks around the farmhouse—feeding the rabbits and geese, hanging out clothes on the line or barbed wire, and ironing with an iron heated on the stove. They learned from their mothers to quilt and darn, which they still do. They learned to refill the gas lanterns, to heat bricks to keep the beds warm on winter evenings, to grind coffee, stoke the fire, put up vegetables for winter, and retrieve the pail of milk hung in the well to keep cool. Today they buy their chickens frozen and wear Woolworth's drip-dry dresses.

As children, many worked outside the home in the fields or factories. One recalled getting lost while picking cotton:

> I was just a bit of a thing then, no more than four or five. I weren't no taller than the cotton. I hollered out for my mother. She couldn't see a thing but the cotton. She took to lookin' down the rows. . . . She found me.

---

* Actually Steinbeck wrote about a much later migration to California. No one in the building came to California in the thirties in the way he describes, although many came from conditions in the Dust Bowl not dissimilar.

Another woman began work at age 11 at a cannery, 12 hours a day for $2.50 paid every two weeks. Toys were improvised out of corn husks or discarded clothes. There was no such thing as play as a "learning experience." Play was something one did in between tasks. The women recall themselves as little rapscallions finding fun in a life of work, drumming on the huge kitchen pots, building little houses from the kindling in the shed, or playing tunes on a comb or blade of grass.

They learned early not only the value of work but the value of thrift. Apple cores were thrown to the pigs, watermelon rinds pickled and preserved, old clothes patched and re-patched, jars saved and reused, broken yarn knotted back together. They still flinch at a wasted bit of food.*

Most families shopped once or twice a year and it was often a day's trip to the nearest large town. As one woman described it:

> We used to live seven miles out. Went shoppin' twice a year, once in the spring to buy some cloth for summer clothes, and once in the fall to get some of that brown domestic to make winter clothes. Don't suppose they have that now. When we got the car, we shopped Saturdays. We used to sit in the car and holler out to friends. We knew everyone then.

Bypassing adolescence, most entered adulthood as teenage brides, parents, and workers. Before children came and after, a majority of the women worked outside the family as cooks, maids, waitresses, and factory hands. Their husbands became carpenters, construction workers, bricklayers, factory hands, rail-

---

* When someone brought watermelon to be eaten in the Recreation Room, it was commented, "What a pity to throw them rinds away. Nobody want the rinds?" No one did, but it was generally agreed that it was a great pity to waste them. One woman whose remark is an emblem of the Protestant Ethic noted emphatically, "I think that's a *sin*." Scraps of cloth were saved to make items for the yearly bazaar, suggesting former ways in which discards were put to use.

road workers, farmers, grocery checkers, stevedores, hospital orderlies, and salesmen.

Three-fourths came to California in the early 1940s seeking high-paying jobs in the shipyards. But almost all the women were laid off in 1945–46 and took jobs in nearby factories, lunch counters, and laundries. A few moved north to farm. After several trips back East, where wages were lower, the climate harsher, and things no longer the same, they returned to California, where most of their children have remained, multiplied, and in a modest way, prospered.

If one were to describe the residents sociologically, one would categorize most of them as rural-born, working-class, white, Anglo-Saxon Protestant widowed females in their late sixties. Although each resident has a unique biography, the broad social categories into which they fall do not distinguish them very much from most other old people of this generation. This study is not based on a random sample and is not representative of a larger population of old people, but the residents are nonetheless not such an unusual group of old people.

Today about 10 percent of the total population is over 65 and most Americans above that age are poor. In 1962 the average income of couples over 65 was $2,804; for widowed or single men it was about half that amount ($1,406) and for widowed or single women it was still less ($982). Most have migrated during their lives from country to city; seven out of ten currently live in urban areas and less than one out of ten on farms. Nationally, over 70 percent were born in the United States.* Over 70 percent report themselves as Protestant, 21 percent as Catholic, and 3 percent as Jewish. Fifty-five percent are female and the older the person the more likely it is that his or her cohorts are female. About two-thirds are widowed or single, and the proportion

---

* Because of the decline in immigration after the early 1900s, the old are more likely than the young to be born in a foreign country. In 1900, 9 percent of the foreign born were over 65 whereas in 1960, 34 percent were. (Bogue, 1959, p. 145; also see Taeuber and Taeuber, 1958.)

widowed is higher for women: at age 65, two-thirds of females and one-third of males have no spouse.* Also, contrary to public opinion, most old people are in fairly good health,** only 2 percent are bedridden and 6 percent housebound.

The residents, like most Americans over 65, were poor. In order to qualify for public housing they had to receive less than $2,800 a year if single and less than $3,000 if married.*** All of them were living on welfare except for a few who received social security and pensions. Only one woman worked, cleaning house and making meals for a blind man in the building. Culturally they came from the stable working class. Although at times they jokingly referred to themselves as "us poor pensioners," they made a sharp distinction between themselves and "poor white trash." Culturally there was a difference. Their granddaughters and daughters wore bouffant hairdos and drove up to visit them in fairly new, large American cars. But at the nearby Baptist church, which some attended regularly, they rubbed shoulders with people who drove in from nearby farms in old trucks and sat at church with unwashed hair and in faded dresses.

The residents, like old people in general, have migrated during their lives from country to city. Merrill Court is also in an urban area, or on the suburban fringe of one. With one exception, all were born in the United States, almost all in the Midwest and Southwest. Ninety percent were Protestant, ten percent were Catholic, and there were no Jews. Of the Merrill Court population of forty-three, only five were men, three married and two single.

---

* At age 85, it goes up to six out of ten males and over eight out of ten females without spouse.

** Most in the community were overweight, as they themselves would remark. However, it wasn't defined as a serious problem since in this company being overweight was normal. (See Burnight and Harden, 1967.)

*** All the residents were white. The housing authority reported that no Blacks had applied for the housing. The same was said to be true of another senior citizen housing project also populated by whites, within the Black community itself. Informal and formal segregation is as true for old as for young Black people.

It could be that a more sociable type of person applied for the housing in the first place. But I asked the residents who originally applied when the housing first opened, and not one mentioned the company it might provide or, for that matter, anything about the social environment. They applied because the rent was cheap ($55 a month) and the apartments new. Later, as apartments were vacated, residents would "speak" for their friends to get them in and this undoubtedly added to the comradeship in the building.

Thus, the residents are not very different from other Americans of their generation. They are slightly untypical in that there are proportionately more women, more widowed, and slightly more Protestant and native born. It is possible that these differences account for the active social life I found there. However, other research shows that widowed people[4] are less likely to have an active social life, and that being female,[5] Protestant, and native born makes one neither more nor less likely to have an active social life. Such flat-footed correlations between characteristics of the individuals (such as age, religion, nativity) and propensity to be active in old age tell us in a rough way only what factors do not seem to explain the burgeoning of this old people's community. There are two remaining factors that I think do account for it. One is the very homogeneity of the group. In the United States of 1972, I doubt whether a group composed of rich and poor or white and black would have had quite the same results. The second is the social context itself, and this is described in Chapter Three.

The Setting

Before we proceed any further, we should look briefly at the background of the town and the housing project in which the subculture developed. Although most of the widows originally migrated from other places, they had lived in California a long time and the history of the town of Verada is as much their history as anyone's, especially as that history reflects a change in ways of dealing with the old.

In 1887 the County Board of Trade put out a pamphlet to attract newcomers to the sparsely populated county:

> Situated as it is, at the very portal of the metropolis of the Pacific, on the great highway of the two transcontinental railways, and at the junction of the two great rivers of the state, Sacramento and San Joaquin, with the soil not excelled by any portion of the state, yielding every product of the semi-tropical and temperate zone; a climate that is almost perfect; sheltered from the harsh winds and fogs of the bay by a coastline of hills, and from the hot blast of the northern wind, by its wide expanse of river tide and marshlands. Here grow, without irrigation or protection, the orange, the olive, the lemon, the pomegranate, the fig, and the grape. Scenery of diversity and grandeur unequalled in all the land . . . (————— County, California, 1887, p. 1.).

Eighty years later, and no longer the home of the orange, the fig, and the grape, the county is part of the suburban sprawl pushing north from the San Francisco Bay area. The main street where the widows shop was once the site of dog races held by gold miners who came periodically down from the hills. Now that street is bordered by neon signs designed to catch the attention of the commuter traffic between the suburbs to the north and the industries and offices to the south. Near four gas stations stands a tiny fountain, the site of one of Lady Bird Johnson's beautification projects.

Before the gold rush days there was a small settlement of Portuguese whalers who before 1908 came mainly from the Azores and after that mainly from the Portuguese mainland. Some stayed in what became Verada to farm and fish, while others moved north to work in the mines and lumber mills. With the gold rush migration from the East, Verada became a honky-tonk town, bounded by little shacks, some of which still stand between the new gas stations and shopping centers. Many gold miners did not find gold but they did find land. In the words of the Board of Trade, ". . . to the man with small means who with a few acres would rear for himself a home where with moderate labor he can earn for himself and family a comfortable support, then this is the country that Providence designed for him." [6]

During World War II, migration from the Midwest, East, and South brought people to Verada not to mine gold but to build ships for war. Looking out from the senior citizen housing, many remember the town then as a vast plain covered with rows of wartime housing and trailers. As one widow recounted:

> From the freeway to Verada Road was all trailer camps. And there was government temporary housing for us shipyard workers. Ya can't recognize the old place now. It's all sprawled out. All kinds of people came then. There was even some convicts down from Nevada to get jobs at Kaiser. We had all kinds of newcomers.

Even staying-put in Verada, the grandmothers have seen so many changes that they might as well have moved. As one pointed out to me, "You know the Super-S on Twenty-third? Used to be a junior high. You know the Bank of America? Used to be a pasture." On nearly every trip home from bowling on Tuesdays the women would comment on what Verada used to look like, "I wonder what happened to that trailer court. I used to live here in the forties. It was a bunch of nice little cabins then." Another mentioned that she used to live where a new motel now stands. Indeed, in the twenty years since the end of World War II, the truck gardens, farm pasture, and war housing had given way to Doggie Diners, bars, gas stations, motels, and modest suburban housing. It lays claim to having more trailer parks per square foot than any other incorporated area in northern California.

The town of Verada, incorporated in 1948, now has a population of 27,000, six elementary schools, two junior highs, and a junior college, which is across the street from Merrill Court. Many of the residents of this blue-collar suburb work for its two major industries, Standard Oil and Bethlehem Steel.

Initially, local religious and independent social groups cared for the old and the bereaved. For example, a social service organization, the *Uniao Portuguesa Do Estado Da California,* taxed the community the sum of $1 on the death of a member and the money was given to the widow and children. The function of such organizations is suggested in the motto of one: "Sociability and Protection." With the growth of the state and nation and the decline of the local community, social security programs have replaced local religious and social groups in caring for the old. The Recreation and Parks Department, set up in 1955, seems to have taken over the "Sociability" function while the Social Welfare Department has taken over "Protection."

The Recreation and Parks Department pays for two half-time salaried positions in the senior citizen housing project. It sends a bus to collect people on voting day and its officials appear on Christmas and Easter. In addition, the Social Welfare Department keeps an eye on the project and most residents receive visits from their social workers. The County Hospital, once run by the church, now asks old-looking people to show their "senior citizen cards." Never before have the residents or their parents or their parents' parents been "senior citizens" to whom tax money was allocated and for whom welfare state professionals were responsible. Clearly the situation for the aged has changed, as has the town, since 1887. But the trend toward special housing for the elderly is recent. As Chapter Two shows, it is only since the 1950s in California that such special public housing has developed. Merrill Court was completed in 1965 with federal, state, county, and private funds. It was named after the private donor.

Thus, in a new apartment building did a collection of old people come together, bringing their histories to a town itself undergoing rapid change. The very lack of stability is itself part of the setting of growing old. That was one of the first lessons I learned about the community life of old people.

chapter two

INTEGRATION
OR SEPARATION

"Give me a staff of honour for mine age,
But not a sceptre to control the world."

Shakespeare,
Titus Andronicus
Act i, scene I, line 198

Along with blacks and women, the old have joined the poor as a "social problem"—a label usually reserved for people who lack power.* We can judge the quality of a society by its "prob-

* Although there is little data on old people in early American society, what studies there have been suggest that old age was not a "social problem" at this time. Frank Furstenberg, in his study of the accounts of foreign travelers in America between 1800 and 1850, found "not a single account discussing the place of old people in the society or even the position of the grandparent in the family" (1966, p. 334.). Furstenberg suggests that this is because the old were only 4 percent of the population. But this is not a compelling explanation since the propor-

lem people"—in this case the old—for it is they who pay the price for what non-problem people enjoy. Although this principle does not operate simply or directly, it is generally true that what a black child does not have is related to what a white child does have and what a poor person does not have is related to what a rich person does have. So too, what an old person does not enjoy is in part related to what a young person does. Where youth is honored, it is generally true that old age is not, and where respect is based on work, lack of work is denigrated. In the case of old age, nearly everyone pays the price in the long run.

The United States, people say, is a youth-oriented society. In fact, I think it puts more premium on the early part of middle age. In itself, without training, skills, or position, youth is a small asset. Of all the "social ages" of life, youth comes closest to the essence of glamor, magic, and power to inspire envy, which we associate with "The American Dream." But youth is only one ingredient. The essence of glamor is the combination of youth with its strength and beauty, with the wealth and recognition that are normally harvested, if at all, in late middle age. (Car ads in *Esquire* and most of the Kennedys suggest such a combination.) Young adulthood comes closest to this combination, while adolescence for one reason, and old age for another, are farthest away from it. In fact, most old people in American society lack both elements and thus they have come to symbolize the exact opposite of, the underside of, the American Dream.

I have said that the old pay for what those in early middle age enjoy. But it is also true that the problems of the old simply exaggerate problems faced by people of all ages. The old recall the feelings we all have at times of being unrewarded, disconnected from what is going on, bypassed and unappreciated. Old people are, most of all, a symbol of powerlessness, not only their own but that of other people. This is one reason why the young,

---

tion of women in society did not increase when they became defined as a "social problem," and similarly with blacks. It may be that a segment of the population becomes a social problem when a high proportion of its norm-*conforming* members experience strain.

and especially persons in late middle age, disassociate themselves from the old and dismiss old age as "depressing."

To most old people themselves, old age is not one social problem but many. There is the problem of poverty, of poor health, and of loneliness. Underlying all three is a condition that is hard to isolate as a "problem," a condition that cannot be changed without radically altering the way resources and honor are distributed. Apart from a privileged elite for whom old age is a harvest of honor and riches, the old in America are not needed by society. This rejection, more than their health or their housing, is the basic problem.

In this chapter and book I will not discuss all the problems of old age, but rather one which I think is crucial—isolation. I think this problem is important for two reasons. First, it has become a sad commonplace to associate being old with being alone. We regard isolation as a punishment for prisoners, but perhaps a majority of American old people are in some degree isolated or fear the prospect of it. To the extent that isolation breeds loneliness and the extent that loneliness is painful, isolation is a serious problem on humanitarian grounds. Old age communities such as the one described here offer an alternative to isolation. Being alone, a person can come to see his problems as individual rather than collective in nature. "Old age consciousness" is an alternative, suggesting as it does collective solutions.

In what follows I will discuss three trends that bear on the problem of isolation: 1) the decline in work for old people, which filters out the old from the society of workers; 2) the development of age-stratification, which puts them in the company of other old people; and 3) the relative weakening of kinship ties, which leads the old to seek supplementary friendships outside the family. In the absence of work and family obligations, residence and the friendships that grow from it become more important. Thus, I will focus on residence in two kinds of contexts—one where old people live near or with young people and one where old people live near or with other old people. I will show, on the basis of other research, how the first generally leads to isolation while the second frequently opens up the possibility of sociability, sometimes community, and even the beginnings of an old age subculture.

Work and Leisure

Despite what some of us hope, there is no sign that more unemployed old people will find work, and many signs that young people also will have a hard time finding it. Although some will probably continue to work as hard as people have ever worked, American society is increasingly supporting, at subsistance level, those who cannot find or do not have jobs. Who works and who does not has all along been a question of social class and race; it is now more and more also a question of age.

In 1900 two out of three men over 65 were working; today less than one-third are. The Bureau of Labor Statistics estimates that only 20 percent will be working in 1980. Moreover, the proportion of older men with full-time work has dropped steadily from 26 percent in 1950 to 15 percent in 1962.* About half the full-time workers are self-employed. Simultaneously, the number over 65 in the total population is steadily increasing.

The old are forerunners of a future leisured society, but this position wins them no status in today's society, which clearly values work most highly. As Hannah Arendt put it, "even the young are part of an emerging society of laborers without labor.[1] Leisure is not quite leisure when you do not have work.** Ironically, the old are more likely than the young to base their

---

* This dramatic decline in the proportion of older workers is much greater than that for any other age group. An interesting exception to this is children and adolescents. The social creation of "adolescence" as a separate stage parallels the social construction of old age as a separate stage of life.
** We should distinguish between high-status leisure (respite from important work), and low-status leisure (non-work). Leisure in itself does not promise the honor suggested in Thorstein Veblen's *The Theory of the Leisure Class.* (See Rosow, 1969).

pride squarely on work. For this generation of old people, leisure unwoven from work, legitimate in its own right, is associated with "recreation," an artifact of the Recreation and Parks Department, and is regarded as "kid-stuff." To many of the old, the "fun ethic" and even the culturally sophisticated use of leisure is an ideological veneer for the growing scarcity of jobs.

If the Protestant Ethic is slowly fading, along with the stage of economic development for which it was appropriate, it probably dies first in the recent generations of adolescents, many of whom, like the old, lack productive roles. But for most young adults today, work is probably only slightly, if at all, less central than it was to their counterparts a generation ago. The legitimacy of leisure partly determines the status of old people,* and that status will remain low until young adults reconsider the link between work and their *own* identity.

Perhaps the central difference between old people now and old people fifty years from now will lie in the meaning of work, and in the distinction between getting paid and being useful, between being useful and feeling worthwhile.[2] When the present youth comes of age, "game day" in the Recreation Room may be no more popular than it is now, but other forms of leisure will be more legitimate.

As a leisured minority, the old have become socially detached from working society. Lacking work, they lack one traditional means by which to build up a pool of acquaintances from which to choose friends. Retirement from work means more of a social loss for the professional class, whose friends are more likely to be work associates, than for the working class, whose friends are more likely to be drawn from the neighborhood. In a society

---

* Other factors determine the status of old people too. The old are poor in a society that values wealth. They are uneducated or miseducated in a society that values relevant education. Their years are numbered in a society that makes capital investment in human beings (e.g., education) with a view to future payoff. Our values thus put a *burden* on old people as a category.

where most adults work, the leisured are left to the company of others with free time.

Age-Stratification

Who works and who has leisure has a great deal to do with one's age, and this is part of a larger pattern. As in the case of students, junior executives, top executives, and retired persons, age and status usually go together. We judge one another with a notion of what status goes with what age: he's old to be a student, young to be a professor, old to marry, young to retire. Some people sometimes are "off time" but most people most of the time "act their age." And there are many rules that make them do so— for example, the age qualifications for working, voting, holding office, getting income tax deductions, being religiously confirmed, drinking, driving a car, marrying, or joining the army. Increasingly, in large bureaucracies especially, age determines when a worker retires, usually at 65. Age may mean different things to different individuals but it means the same thing to the organization, and this reacts back on the individual and his social life.

People of the same status tend to associate with one another so that a society stratified by status is a society stratified by age. The old, because they tend to occupy similar status, are bound to the old, the middle aged to the middle aged, the young adult to the young adult, and the teenager to the teenager. To be sure, bonds across age barriers exist, but current trends in American social institutions weaken them. We expect to see young and old separated from each other in clubs and cliques, on park benches, in school rooms, offices, factories, surgical and pediatric hospital wards, and in the various rooms of a large church on Sunday. In fact, age-stratification has come to seem so "normal" that it is difficult to detect it.

It is not new. Probably never in American history has it

been true that friendships were randomly distributed across the age spectrum. Alexis de Tocqueville, Geoffrey Gorer, Margaret Mead, and David Riesman have commented on the horizontal age-slicing traditional to American life. Gorer, for example, points out that for adolescents, the authority of the parent is replaced by the authority of the peer group. "With rare exceptions . . . the children of a play group are very much of an age. . . . This group of near equals is in many ways the primary group for Americans all their lives; it is against these that they must measure and prove themselves." [3] After adolescence, the pattern persists: "Most Americans after marriage replace the friendly-competitive group of age mates by their present nearest rivals—their business or professional associates, and often their neighbors, the parents of their children's friends." [4] And this pattern continues on into old age.

If age-stratification has for some time seemed "normal," there are trends both in the economy and the family that strengthen it. [5] There has been a gradual growth of large, internally specialized bureaucracies that divide and deal with people according to status, and thus age. For example, the grandmothers of Merrill Court recall going to small country schools that grouped children aged six to fourteen in one room. Its large urban counterpart separates children by grade and age. In the small rural churches they attended, young children, middle-aged adults, and old sat together in the congregation. In its large modern counterpart there is a nursery, a grade school group, a teenage group, and a senior citizen group. The grandmothers remember nothing like the stores that specialize in children's or teenagers' goods where they now shop for their grandchildren. They recall no speech unique to adolescents then, although they notice it among their teenaged grandchildren today. (One grandmother, in response to a question, said, "Back then people were watchful. Today you're out of sight—I don't mean that the way my granddaughter does.") Today some institutions, such as a university, specialize in late adolescence, while other institutions, such as senior citizen public housing projects, specialize in old age.

Those organizations that specialize in dealing with people of one age bracket have grown more important now, and small organizations that were not formerly stratified by age now are. Furthermore, age-specialization *inside* these bureaucracies has expanded *outward* into informal non-institutional settings. Thus, the status conferred on an individual by such institutions carries over into other settings, so that informal gatherings, neighboring patterns, and friendships outside institutions increasingly resemble those inside them.

Family and Kinship

As bureaucracies have grown stronger, the family has in some ways weakened. Kinship ties have always bound together people of different ages. But as kinship ties have declined as a force,* relatives of different ages are less tied to one another. The functions the family used to perform have been transferred to specialized agencies outside the family, and these agencies, such as the school and the nursing home, tend to deal with people on the basis of their age. Of course, even within the kinship circle, people of an age often group together, as American sociologist Herbert Gans points out in his book *The Urban Villagers.* But only with the decline of kinship ties can full age subcultures with their own institutions, their own customs and folklore, develop.

Along with the decline of kinship ties, several demographic trends have ripened conditions for the growth of old age and adolescent subcultures. On the whole, people can expect to live longer than they could sixty years ago, and thus their marriages tend to last longer. At the same time, there has been a long-range decline in fertility and a closer spacing of children, so that parenthood takes a shorter period of the marriage and of life. There is more looking forward to it and back at it. The post-

---

* Scholars have recently disputed this point. When asked whether they thought kinship ties were as important now as they used to be, a majority of the Merrill Court residents said "no."

parental period in particular has become a new stage* of life, in which the old, like adolescents, are more on their own. They are less tied down and less tied *in*, more vulnerable to the process of atomization and more receptive to the communal responses to it. Like adolescents, the old are more or less freed of the parent-child bond and available for liaisons with people their own age.

These developments leave the nuclear family, stripped from both ends, open to the forces that divide people by status and age. Age-stratification moves into the social vacuum that the family has left, loosening but not eliminating continuity between the generations.

Thus, two trends, the decline in work for old people and the growth of age-stratification, combine with a third trend, the decline in importance of kinship. The first limits the friendships of old people to others with leisure; the second limits them to others their own age; and the third makes them seek supplemental friendships outside the narrowing and looser kinship circle. These trends isolate the old but they also allow what a stronger kinship system once prevented,[6] an elaboration of subcultures based on age.

The subcultures of old age and adolescence share something in common. Like adolescents, old people share not only their biological age but the social position that normally goes with it. As I have mentioned, they are marginal to the economy and in varying degrees separate from the family, although they are not defined in relation to any institution in the way school defines adolescence. But in both cases, to handle a period of transition, a sub-culture has developed. In neither case are all those who are eligible for it in the subculture, and versions of that subculture vary from one locale to another.

The old age subculture in some instances approaches a rear-guard counter-culture, different from and opposed to the main-

---

* In 1890 the last child married an average of two years after the death of one of the parents. In 1950 the last child is married thirteen to fourteen years before the death of one parent. (Glick, 1957.)

stream of society in its value of old-fashioned ways; its common rootedness in a more rural, agrarian, small-town; more ethnically divided America; in its political awareness formed by earlier historic events and its memory for old tunes, dress styles, and cooking. In some ways the old age counter-culture is, ironically, more counter to current social trends than is the young counter-culture whose customs, if not basic values, are quickly assimilated by the mass media and urban-educated sectors of mainstream society.

The Social Integration and Separation of Old People

These three trends isolate the old from family and work, and from young people outside the family. And if these trends continue, the choice for old people will increasingly be between isolation or social involvement with other old people. As the workplace becomes less important as a source of friendships, neighborhood becomes more important.* A look at residential patterns will show how these two choices for old people are sociologically shaped.

American old people today live in two main kinds of residential settings: integrated (young and old living together in the same family or neighborhood) and separated (old people living together in the same residence or neighborhood). I will discuss why the first, more common, and accepted setting often leads to social isolation and why the second, newer and less generally approved, fosters sociability. Since the layman's image** of these

---

* Neighborhood is more important to old people in the lower class than in the middle class.
** On a questionnaire on attitudes toward old age given to 105 freshmen and sophomores in an Introductory Sociology class and Social Problems class at the University of California, Berkeley, in the spring of 1968, I found that 56 percent of the respondents thought "most old people prefer friends their own age." On the other hand, only 19 per-

two contexts may distort the real picture, I will briefly discuss the images as well as the actuality of each context.

Although I will not go into it now, we should also bear in mind the many smaller more subjective social worlds within these objective contexts. A widowed grandmother living with her children can *feel* very isolated. The old person living in the midst of a busy social life of a retirement community may not know a soul. The context is one thing and what an individual makes of it is another. For the purposes of this chapter, however, I am assuming a rough link between the objective context and the subjective experience of it.

Integration

Most age-integrated contexts in the United States today are in small and dwindling ethnic communities or rural enclaves where kinship ties have remained strong, within a larger society that is increasingly stratified by age. But when one searches for an example of an old person *living* together with his children, grandchildren, and assorted relatives, the mind moves to other times and places—to the grandfather in Thomas Mann's novel *Buddenbrooks,* for example. Set in nineteenth-century Germany, the grandfather lived, worked, commanded, protected, bequeathed, and finally died in the heart of the Buddenbrook family.

Thomas Buddenbrook was a powerful man, not a social problem. It was by virtue of him that cousins and aunts and uncles were together and their relationships to one another counted. Three generations of the immediate family lived together in a large house, and every second week by custom all members of the extended family living in town assembled for dinner. Thomas was not isolated from the young, not set apart in

---

cent agreed, "It would probably be better if most old people lived in residences or neighborhoods with people their own age." Thus they accepted the idea of age-horizontal relations—or believed that old people want them—but did not accept the idea of age-separation.

a social pool of unrelated older people.* For him, biological death and social retirement more or less coincided, so that his old age merely continued the life he knew in what is now the "middle" age.

But social conditions were different there and then. In the United States today only about 8 percent of people over 65 live with their children and grandchildren, and probably no more than this ever did in the past.[7] About a fourth to a third of old people now live with an adult child (but not grandchild.)** A widowed grandmother may move in with her daughter and son-in-law or a divorced man may live on with his mother and father. But it has been rare, and since World War II it has become rarer,*** to see two generations of intact marriages living together.

More frequently, old people live alone or with friends who are not related. This does not mean that the old are cut off from their children: 84 percent of American old people live less than an hour away from a child. But typically they do not live together.

And more important, most old people do not *want* to live with their children. Many who do live with them do so because

---

* He was functionally and socially integrated into his social setting, which itself fit smoothly into the larger society. A similar image, modified and Americanized, is found in Willa Cather's "Neighbor Rosicky" (1956). Here the old man is not quite patriarchal but he is still a man whose authority is not much weakened by the years, whose opinion is still sought, whose skills are valued; and he is surrounded by his family to the end.

** One national study of old people in three countries showed that about two-thirds of those with living children see one child as often as every day or two days. This includes old people who live with children in the same household (which the author estimates at 28 percent in the U.S.). (Stehouwer, 1965; Riley and Foner, 1968, p. 542.)

*** Roughly half (53 percent) of those over 65 live as married couples and roughly half do not. Of that 53 percent, 38 percent live with their spouse alone, 12 percent live with spouse and a child, and 3 percent with spouse and others. Of those who do not live as a married couple, 20 percent live alone, 16 percent are single parents living with a child, and 11 percent live with other persons.

it saves money, not because it is a good social arrangement. Less than 10 percent of a recent national sample of old people said they wanted to live with a child or relative. Only 17 percent recommended it to other old people able to care for themselves. Even for ill or disabled old people, more (39 percent) recommended going to a nursing home or getting nursing care than recommended moving in with children (23 percent).[8]

Many of the Merrill Court residents have lived at some point with their children, and most of them now prefer not to. Once in a gathering of the widows, one said, "It would suit me just fine if I had all my family under one roof." But a chorus of others countered; "It wouldn't work for long." "Each generation has to live its own way." "It didn't work with my parents either." This does not mean that family life is unimportant to the widows or to their counterparts among the old. Paradoxically, family life becomes, if anything, more important than before. That is one reason they give for living separately; they want relations to be "good," and this seems to involve a special kind of generational autonomy.

Many young people feel the same way. According to a survey I did of students in two sociology classes at the University of California, Berkeley, in 1968, only a small proportion (7 percent) expected their aged parents to live with them, and only 3 percent expected to live with their own adult children. (Even in the counter-culture, communes are usually composed of people the same age, generally under 30.)

The dilemma with the age-integrated setting of the Buddenbrook family transplanted to the United States is this: the trend toward leisure, toward increasing age-stratification and the loosening of kinship ties in the United States, does not foster age-integration. To realize this image in twentieth-century America would mean to change not only the context, but the very structure of American society.

To a great extent, the same holds true for age-integrated friendships in neighborhoods. When the old live alone or as a couple near young people *outside* the family, they usually do not make friends with them. In fact, an old person with young neighbors is often more isolated than his peer who lives near other old people. In a very important and excellent study of Cleveland residents, sociologist Irving Rosow[9] compared 1,200 old people living in three kinds of housing: one with a mix of ages ("normal"), one with quite a few old people ("age concentrated"), and one with almost all old people ("age dense"). Those living with many other old people made the most friends. But even in the normal neighborhoods (with about 12 percent old people), most befriended not young people but others their own age. If one has other old people around, as in "dense" housing, it expands the circle of potential friends, whereas if one lives mainly with young people, the circle tends to contract. Finally, a study of 500 old people in Elmira, New York, showed that the older a widow, the less isolated she was, since she was less likely to be the only widow on the block and more likely to have (other widow) friends.[10]

These data mean that the more "segregated" the neighborhood itself, the more integrated the old person is *within* it. One survey of older clients of five social agencies in Schenectady, New York, showed that of those needing rehousing, 60 percent did not want to live in a neighborhood with small children.[11] In another case, a retirement public apartment building reserved a third of its units for younger families in order to stimulate friendships across the age barrier. Out of eighty-eight friendships reported, only one old person made friends with a young person. A subsequent study sampling the old in the same housing unit checked this point again and found that of all the old people's neighbor friends, only 4 percent were young.

A mutual lack of interest between young and old can, in varying degree, isolate the old. A retired couple living in the same neighborhood with a young couple with small children does not go to the same school board meetings or share the same attitude toward lawns, dogs, or noise. Under these circumstances, the old can become an alien minority amidst their young neighbors. Even when the old live under the same roof with their own children, similar problems, for the same reasons, emerge. Simply to juxtapose old and young is not to assure something in common. It is to offer the trappings of social integration without the social foundations for it.

Not all old people are like the widow in the British film, *The Whisperers,** living alone in a musty flat with only a radio and cat for company. More typical is the "emancipated" older couple living on their own, separate from their children in neighborhoods with young working neighbors. But this situation, too, can easily dissolve into isolation. Each member of the couple has a fair chance of being alone within a few years. At age 65, already 55 percent are widowed or single—30 percent of the men and 70 percent of the women. Poor health and death gradually steal away those special long-term friendships, and retirement narrows the circle of acquaintances that, on hindsight, rested on having work in common.

Age-integration in the family or neighborhood, although never a dominant pattern, has declined. If it continues to decline and if no other neighborhood context appropriate to the newer age-stratification emerges, the result will be increasing isolation of old people. One alternative to this outcome is residential contexts mainly for old people.

Separation

Today in the United States old people live together in a number of places: private retirement villages for the well-to-do, public housing for the poor, some unplanned old people's suburbs, or the fringes of downtown commercial districts. The downtown hotels for old people are really examples of *de facto segregation,*

---

* Her only human encounters are with a hostile young neighbor, a well-meaning social worker, an exploitative young stranger, a polite but distant son, and an estranged husband. Otherwise she is alone, although surprisingly unlonely.

but the term, "separation" better describes the planned retirement housing that residents have chosen over other alternatives. I will talk about some research on these contexts before describing one in particular.

Although old people (10 percent of the population) live in independent housing in age-integrated neighborhoods, they are only 3 percent of the population in some new suburbs and 30 percent in cities such as St. Petersburg, Florida. Since World War II, there has been a mushroom growth of old age housing, drop-in centers, and retirement settlements such as Ryderwood in Washington State, Moosehaven in Florida, Sun City (which has over 12,000 residents) in Arizona, and the Rossmoor Leisure Worlds in California.

Unlike the image of Buddenbrook in his family or the lonely widow is a new archetype—the sociable, tanned, older couple given to organized shuffleboard tournaments, bingo parties, and a life of busy leisure. Here an old person is not integrated with the young but neither is he isolated. He may even find a new mate. One study found that almost a third of the married couples in a retirement community had met and married there.

Many outsiders feel ambivalent toward these new old age subcultures, partly because they are based on leisure and partly because they separate the old from the young. It may suggest to them the pseudo-identity of "senior citizens," contrived devices to "keep active" though not useful, to be busy without being needed or having power. It also suggests a break in generational ties. However, there is nothing *inherent* in communities of people of the same age that requires a title like "senior citizen" or the activities often associated with it. Furthermore, as Chapter V shows, having old friends can enhance family relations rather than compete with them.

Age-separation in no way alters the basic conditions discussed earlier. On the other hand, the old in such communities do have functions and power *within* the retirement subculture that itself is cut off from the main culture. They have status within that subculture although it is a status that loses in the translation to the outside culture.

Studies on a variety of age-separated communities suggest that they reduce the isolation of old people. One study in Arizona, comparing people in age-integrated communities with people in age-separated communities, found that the latter had more friends and "higher morale."[12] A comparison between lower-class residents of a public housing project similar to Merrill Court and a control group of rejected applicants for the same housing showed the same pattern. Each individual in the senior citizen public housing was matched on seven traits with a rejected applicant still in private housing (and not living with other old people). Those residents of public housing were more likely to have friends, to join organizations, and to be active.[13] According to virtually all the research on attitudes of residents in old age communities, they like living together with other older people.

There is a well-known theory in gerontology called the theory of disengagement.[14] According to it, as people grow older, they reduce ties to the outside world and invest less emotion in the ties they retain.* In doing so they gradually "die" socially before they die biologically. This process, according to the theory, is "natural" and is linked to the nearness to death. The research cited in this chapter and my own field work suggest that this theory describes nothing "natural" but merely what happens *under certain social conditions.* Old people living among peers are much less likely to disengage, to isolate themselves, or to be isolated.

---

* According to the theory, as disengagement proceeds, the "web of normative control" within which we normally live grows weaker. Being with people one cares about and whose opinions one values, tends to make one conform to the little niceties of life. People who eat alone are more likely to eat with their fingers, and this process may affect the larger things in life as well. The oddities one sees, the old lady in the bizarre hat or inside-out raincoat, so well illustrated by Dame Edith Adams in *The Whisperers*, might show up in the behavior of anyone of any age who lives alone.

A Case in Point

Within these two broad types of integrated and separated housing are many smaller social worlds—the Merrill Court public housing project for example. It is not isolated nor part of a self-sufficient old age settlement,* but is in an urban area, close to many of the families of the residents. The question I would like to ask is this: What about this context seems to prevent social isolation? After all, there is no *necessary* link between an apartment house full of individuals over 62 years of age and a community. What made it a *community?* I have already suggested in Chapter One that it is not the particular social or personal characteristics of the people who happen to live there. In Chapter Three I will answer this question by looking at the history of Merrill Court. I would like to answer it in a different way here. The life of one voluntarily *un*sociable resident, an 80-year-old farmer's widow named Daisy, reveals a good deal about the persistent social pressures toward sociability and away from isolation.

Since Daisy did not come down to the Recreation Room very often, I visited her two or three times a week in her apartment. She usually sat in a chair by her window and stared out most of the day, sewing, or watching television, stirring only to clean the apartment, fix herself food, and occasionally go out visiting or shopping. She had been in and out of the hospital several times, returning each time a bit weaker than the time before. This was the picture her neighbors had of her, it was how she described herself, and it was how she seemed to me. When I dropped in for a visit, Daisy would smile, talk about her past, and make a few polite inquiries about "what was goin' on

---

* In general, age-separated contexts work best if they are either linked in some way to the wider society or if they are large enough to be clearly self-sustaining. Settlements that are extremely isolated and inaccessible and are not large enough to be commercially self-sustaining tend to present a gloomier picture.

downstairs." When told, she expressed mild interest, much as she was mildly interested in the lives of her children.

But Daisy was not left alone in the buzz of activity. Two women on her floor appointed themselves her informal "protectors." One walked by her window every morning to see if the curtains were drawn; the other came in the afternoon and evening, and both reported on her welfare to the rest of the group. As one protector commented, "That's how we do here, to make sure everthing's all right."

Downstairs and in the privacy of their apartments, the residents expressed definite opinions about Daisy. As one put it, "Daisy doesn't want to be down gadding about with us. She likes being upstairs, just sittin'. What's the use of living if you're not up to somethin'?" * Daisy was gently chastised for not coming down to the potluck dinners on Fridays. She claimed that she was on a salt-free diet, but, as the others brought out, there was salt-free food downstairs. When she still declined, they brought some up to her, for which they were mildly thanked. The group knew the details of Daisy's physical ailments, as they did those of almost everyone in the building, and they made assessments about how much of her inactivity was due to physical decline and how much was not. The consensus was that she could be more sociable if she wanted.

What is important here is that Daisy, as a "drop out," was deviant within what is as yet a deviant subculture of old people. Within this pool of sociability, the problem was not isolation, but, if anything, social pressure preventing a recluse from feeling comfortable.

There was not only social pressure to keep active and involved, but social pressure to "be proper." In this respect,

---

* It was said about a similar widow: "She lives with her feet up. Says the doctor told her not to walk; now nobody believes her. That's acting old when you ain't." And another said, "I don't see why she doesn't do anything. I told her, I said, 'Lucy, you've gotten into a rut.' And she'll say back, 'I know I have' but she won't make a move. She wants people to come to her. I talk to her but you can only push a person so far."

Beatrice was deviant. Most of the residents were brought up as fundamentalist Baptists in the rural Midwest, mainly Oklahoma and Arkansas, and they strongly disapprove of drink. Beatrice, on the other hand, used to run what she called an "after hours motel" in West Virginia, and, as she put it, "I used to be kinda easy on the eye. Men gave me a lot of presents, and we had a good time, ya know. Things are kind of slow around here." Beatrice drinks and has men up to her room occasionally. She wears diamond earrings and tight-fitting pants to morning workshops. She seldom offers her time for a bake sale and refuses any office that has responsibility attached. She normally comes down to the Recreation Room only when there is food and leaves before the dishes are done. She doesn't help the more disabled members of the community with their shopping, although her daughter has one of the few cars, and she seldom goes to other people's funerals.

Beatrice, like Daisy, is a deviant within the community.* She is a social litmus paper for the social constraints on the behavior of *all* the members. The gossip about her is a potent reminder of what could happen to anyone who so blatantly disregards the group's conventions. Disapproval of her is perhaps the only topic on which nearly everyone agrees. Many want to ostracize Beatrice from the Service Club, to which she owes back dues, but hesitate because she is the only good piano player. (She plays tinpanny tunes that she learned from her motel days.)

Outside such a community,** the Beatrices of the world

* It is hard to know whether or not she was a deviant back in West Virginia, and whether in fact she cares less now about what other people think than she ever did. The point is that her resistance to social pressure is itself an exception in the group. The communal reaction to her behavior is a good example of Kai Erikson's notion of boundary maintenance. (Erikson, 1966.)

** This community was what one might call "tight." A common topic of conversation among the residents was other people's behavior. On a typical morning in the Recreation Room, discussion moved from what Dolly had on today when she went shopping to what Mrs. Martin ate for dinner, to whether it was appropriate to wear hats to church or curlers to the doctor's office. If a resident broke the rules by wearing might be tolerated or ignored, just as the Daisy's might be put in institutions at the first sign of failing. Within such a community, Beatrice and Daisy define the social borders. The values of activism, productivity, and propriety may be peculiar to this group and to this generation of old people. But the ways in which such values integrate a group is not unique to them. Beatrice and Daisy may seem like casualties of coercive sociability, but if this is a problem and I see it as a minor one, then it must be measured against the equally enforced isolation of older people outside such a context. Old age communities in housing projects such as this are an alternative to isolation. There are many kinds of old age communities, but the rest of the book is about this one in particular, which I think works.

---

a hat to church or curlers to the doctor's office, she normally felt it necessary to explain why.

There was also a newly remarried couple, Mr. and Mrs. Farmer, who live on the first floor of the apartment house. In my three years of field work, the door to their apartment was never anything but ajar from 8:00 A.M. to around 5:30 P.M. Mrs. Farmer (the club treasurer) acts as the functional "sphincter" of the building. She watches and reports on those who come into and go out of the building. The couple moved into the building the month it opened in 1965 and they initially refused to unlock the main door for other occupants because they "didn't know who they were."

chapter three

AN OLD AGE COMMUNITY

Mrs. Clark's Typical Day:

"(Morning) I get up about seven in the morning. Then I fix a little breakfast and have my breakfast. Then I clean the dishes and start in cleaning the house. Dust, scrub, washin' and just general house-cleaning. Sometimes I wash or iron and do things like that.

(Afternoon) A little before noon I prepare a little lunch. I usually have lunch about noon. I clean the dishes, and if I can, I gad about. I usually visit (a relative). Sometimes I just watch TV or sometimes I straighten things around the house.

(Evening) I usually prepare a little supper to have it ready by about five. Then I wash the dishes and usually watch TV the rest of the evening." *

> "Utterly boring. I certainly hope that won't be my typical day at 69."
>
> "She's in a rut. She should get involved in the community around her. Why doesn't she do something constructive?"
>
> "It's kind of wasteful, but if that's what she wants to do—let her do her own thing." **

Evolution of a Subculture

Most of the widows who moved into Merrill Court had lost their husbands within the last five years. Aside from five who knew one another casually, the widows were strangers before 1965.[1]

* From *Growing Old: The Process of Disengagement,* by Elaine Cumming and William Henry, Basic Books, Inc., Publishers, New York, 1961.
** Selected questionnaire responses, Sociology I Class, University of California, Berkeley, Spring 1968.

The story of how a collection of near-strangers became a community has several versions. Almost from the start, there was a structure of parallel leadership, as in the nineteenth-century British and French colonies. As Freda, the first "indigenous" leader tells it, "There wasn't nothin' before we got the coffee machine. I mean we didn't share nothin' before Mrs. Bitford's daughter brought over the machine and we sort of had our first occasion, you might say." There were about six people at the first gathering around the coffee machine in the Recreation Room. As people came downstairs from their apartments to fetch their mail in mid-morning, they looked into the Recreation Room, found a cluster of people sitting down drinking coffee, and some joined in. A few weeks later the Recreation Director "joined in" for the morning coffee, and as she tells it, the community had its start at this point. She had formerly worked at a bowling alley nearby and, as she put it:

> I went to see Ted at the alleys and I worked out a special season rate for the seniors. We organized teams and always got Lanes 6 and 7 from 2 to 3 on Tuesdays. People actually got to know each other bowling. I drove them there and back and at the end of the year we had a "do" for the winning team and the best bowler.

Half a year later Merrill Court was a beehive of activity: meetings of a Service Club, which was soon set up; bowling; morning workshop; Bible study classes twice a week; monthly birthday parties; and visits to four nearby nursing homes. Members donated cakes, pies, and soft drinks to bring to the nursing home, and a five-piece band, including a washtub bass, played for the "old folks" there. The band also entertained at a nearby recreation center for a group of Vietnam veterans. During afternoon band practice, the women sewed and embroidered pillow cases, aprons, and yarn dolls. They made wastebaskets out of discarded paper towel rolls, wove rugs from strips of old Wonder Bread wrappers, and Easter hats out of old Clorox bottles, all to be sold at the annual bazaar. They made placemats to be used at the nursing home, tote-bags to be donated to "our boys in Vietnam," Christmas cards to be cut out for the Hillcrest Junior Women's Club, rag dolls to be sent to the orphanage, place cards to be written out for the bowling league banquet, recipes to be written out for the recipe book that was to go on sale next month, and thank you and condolence cards.

All this activity had a special meaning for the widows. Through it they defined what was work and what was leisure, what was "on" time and what was "off" time. This meaning could easily be lost in a behaviorist study. A behaviorist doing research[2] at Merrill Court might note the following. At 9:00 o'clock, one woman entered the Recreation Room, gathered materials, and began making yarn dolls. At 9:10, two other women entered the room, sat down, and did the same. Within half an hour, nine or ten others were assembled at the table, cutting pieces of yarn, wrapping and tying them into different shapes, and putting them in a large pile. One woman with a lame arm, who had been sitting and watching, was handed some of the finished dolls, which she wrapped with one hand. The women looked at one another, talked, laughed, and continually handled the yarn. One woman patted two others on the back. Another entered the room, was hugged and kissed, took off her coat, and began to handle the yarn. At 10:00 o'clock two got up, made coffee, and served it to the rest. At 10:30 they all went out to the mail room and returned with letters. Several read their letters aloud. One woman began singing and was watched while the others continued handling the yarn. At noon, four or five women left the room and returned with dishes of food.

What was going on? What meaning did this activity have for the people involved? Was it work or was it leisure? All the women were living on social welfare, social security, or pensions, and in the eyes of society they were not workers. They earned no pay and had no employer, paid no taxes, and punched no time clocks. They came to the Recreation Room voluntarily and a decision to come downstairs to work was a decision about what to do with their leisure. But if you asked them, they would tell you they were working. They jokingly talked about being on "company time" and talked about what they would do when they were "free" to attend to their own affairs. It was written into the weekly schedule on the bulletin board as "workshop" and if one of the regulars failed to come down, she was called and reminded. If people came only to talk, they were quietly handed work.

I should say at this point that what follows is not written from a behaviorist perspective, since the focus of this study is not on behavior *per se* but on its meanings. In particular, it focuses on the meaning of roles and relationships—the formal ones downstairs and the informal ones upstairs; the ones at the top of the social ladder and the ones at the bottom; the ones based on earned status and the ones based on "luck" status. Having described these, I will then play back over the descriptions, showing how they illustrate aspects of the special "sibling bond" that emerged between social equals and that forestalls the isolation of the old, discussed in Chapter Two.

Thus, the morning's activities downstairs meant work. The residents also described them as "enjoyable," but the enjoyment was incidental to getting the yarn dolls finished and ready to sell at the annual bazaar. The money from the sale was used to "have fun" seeing a movie or the Ice Follies, dining out, or touring California. The official principle was "work now to have fun later." Yet the work itself was interspersed with eating, talking, and (as the woman in the behavioral description above was doing), singing ballads.

Strung on this web of sociability, then, was a value on work, on being productive. Even the dead, once they were gone, were evaluated according to their work. For example, when one widow died, people mentioned that she had worked all year on the bazaar and had died just before the trip to the Ice Follies. They regretted her absence but posthumously praised her for being "such a good worker," not for her ability to enjoy things. Irma, a farmer's widow from West Texas, compared the work downstairs to an old-fashioned "workin' in." As she put it,

Neighbors would come in and help out if you were takin' in a harvest or doin' some cannin'. One time our barn burned down and we had another one up in two days. Doin' it together we got more done, see? I met my husband at a workin' in.*

Other occasions were for "pure" fun. There were, for example, the parties to celebrate birthdays, Thanksgiving, Christmas, Easter, Halloween; and there was some dispute about what to do with St. Patrick's Day. By the third year there was a potluck luncheon every other week for residents only and on alternate weeks, luncheons for outsiders. Following the potluck dinners there were post-potluck luncheons to use up leftovers. Also, food salesmen, kitchenware sellers, hobby experts, and hairdressers came to demonstrate their goods. After the demonstrations, tin-working or basket-weaving classes might be established, only to disband a month or so later. Once a week there was "Recreation Day," which was called "Game Day" until objections were voiced: "That sounds like kid stuff. We're not children, you know." On this day they played card games such as Cheat Your Neighbor, Aggravation, or Canasta. Only eight were regular players. A number did not play because "their religion was against it," although they would nonetheless sit on the sidelines each week making comments to that effect: "I never played a game of cards nor touched a drop of liquor." **

Both work and play were somebody's responsibility to organize. The Merrill Court Service Club, to which most of the residents and a half-dozen non-residents belonged, set up committees and chairmanships that split the jobs many ways. There was a group of permanent elected officials: the President, Vice-President, Treasurer, Secretary, and a Birthday Chairman, in

---

* They talked over the possibility of having a "workin'-in" to can some peaches, which one of the sons of a resident had brought in. But, as they complained, sugar cost too much and they had thrown out the jars when they moved into the small apartments.
** Mr. Farmer, for example, stated that "his" God was against card playing, although, as everyone pointed out, he was an avid pool player. Freda, who attended the same Southern Baptist church, did permit herself a game of cards.

addition to the Recreation Director. Each activity also had a chairman and each chairman was in charge of a group of volunteers. Offices that were rotated during the year included the Chairman of the Flower Fund, Chairman of Publicity, "Sunshine" Chairman (who sent out condolence and get-well cards), "Secret Pal" Chairman (who arranged for gifts to be given anonymously on birthdays and at Christmas), and the Chairman of the Bowling League banquet. Only four club members did not chair some activity between 1965 and 1968; and at any time about a third were in charge of something. There was an annual election of officers by secret ballot followed by installation of officers—the biggest affair of the year. Outgoing officers usually stood up to accept a long round of applause; and those who had been applauded became, in time, vigorous applauders.

Issues

As activities gradually became more communal, certain customs, in competition with others, became known as "our way" of doing things. Consensus on what was "our way" was questioned only when an issue arose; or rather, a disagreement became an issue when it was unclear whose side others would take.

For example, Ada, a former shipyard cleaning woman in World War II and an acknowledged hard worker, was making wastebaskets. She made them from discarded paper towel rolls that the residents donated and with glue, paint, and scissors that the Recreation Department donated. The wastebaskets were to be sold at the annual bazaar, the proceeds of which went to the Service Club's kitty (called "mad money"), which in turn financed the members' excursions. An issue arose when Ada asked if she could keep two of the twenty baskets she had made, to give her children for Christmas. Ernestine, a Canadian carpenter's wife, complained: "I've knitted twelve pairs of socks and I gave every one to the bazaar. If we all took what we made, there'd be a small heap to sell. How far could we get on that kind of money?" Every day for a week thereafter conversations usually got around to "Ada's basket problem." Some people, especially those who made items for the bazaar, sympathized with the aggrieved, and others did not. The issue questioned the boundary between public and private property, between public and private time.

The solution—that the baskets were public property—was at first accepted only by the five important officers. After an incubation period, during which other opinions were privately assessed, a tentative consensus emerged. Only after the bazaar and the trip following it did most others come around on the issue. By the time of the next bazaar, the principle "What you make here is public property" was not publicly questioned and the issue had, in the meantime, fallen into the realm of recent tradition: "We've always done it that way." *

Other issues—such as whether or not to have formal bylaws, whether to keep the Club's money in a cigar box in the Treasurer's apartment or whether to put it in the bank, whether chairs could be borrowed from the Recreation Room by other organizations without permission, whether non-dues-paying members could go on trips, whether a 40-year-old woman who came to meetings could join the Club, at what age to set the limit for membership, how many potlucks to restrict to residents only— all seemed to follow the same course on the way to becoming precedents.

Whose opinion counted most depended on who knew the most, cared the most, and had the most elaborate suggestions. Only a few had been more than casually involved in voluntary

---

* Ada did not come down to meetings for a month but she finally rejoined the group, although privately she felt the decision unjust. A number of issues seemed to jeopardize collective life and highlight the importance of quasi-private friendship networks. When a hot issue remained unsettled, the public norm that "everyone is welcome here" in the Recreation Room was substituted by, "This table is reserved for our close friends." Thus, issues affected the fluctuating boundary between private and public, formal and informal, status arrangements.

clubs before coming to Merrill Court. These few "old hands" became the culture-carriers from one (age-integrated) sector of society to another (age-separated) sector. Not only she who had experience but she who advocated the most elaborate and official-seeming ritual usually won her point. For example, what was to happen at the yearly Installation of Officers banquet was not entirely a settled matter even by the third year. Harriet, a widow from Wisconsin, suggested to the group a few months before the affair:

> Why don't we have Floyd circle once around and usher Freda (the outgoing officer) to her seat. Then he can circle once around and usher Delia (the incoming President) to the front where Freda was sitting. It looks real nice. That's the way the VFW (Veterans of Foreign Wars) does.

There were a few supportive remarks ("If that's how they do it, that's how it's supposed to be done." and "It looks right to me.") Some suggestions were made about the number of circles Floyd was to make and from which side Freda was to exit and Delia to enter before the ritual settled into people's memories. The few who opposed the "hocus pocus" were reminded that Harriet "knew about these things," and they did not care enough to object.[3] In the same way, details about signing the guest book, handling coats, seating people, and rising for the flag were suggested by a voluntary cultural advisor and ratified by the group. Thus was the social architecture gradually built up and passed into the realm of things "as they have always been." The prehistory of these customs is vague in almost everyone's mind and no one takes responsibility or credit for them now.

In his analysis of secret societies, the German sociologist Georg Simmel made an interesting comparison of the late-nineteenth-century American and German Freemasons. In the United States, where the individual enjoyed relative freedom in the general society, Freemasonry had the most rigorous internal rules and rituals. In Germany, where there was less freedom in the general society, the lodges were internally freer of ritual and more independent from one another. Simmel concluded that man

> . . . needs a certain ratio between freedom and law . . . when he does not receive it from one source, he seeks to supplement what he obtains of the one by the missing quantity of the other, no matter from what additional source, until he has the ratio he needs.[4]

The ritual of Freemasonry is itself, as Simmel points out, objectively often senseless, but it fills a social void.

In society at large, what old people ought or ought not to do is only vaguely defined. The former "should's" and "shouldn't's" that applied to a wife, a worker, or a mother have faded with time. But this was clearly not the case in Merrill Court. If one was no longer a mother to a brood of small children, or a wife, or provider, one was at least the Birthday Chairman or the Treasurer or a member of the Flower Committee. For friends lost through death there were replacements; whenever an apartment was vacated, it was immediately filled by the first on a long list of applicants at the housing agency. If there was no longer work that "had to be done," something like it was there. With each new role came new customs and new notions of the right and wrong of them.

At least in the case of old people, Simmel's fixed ratio of freedom to constraint holds only under certain conditions. The neatly carved roles and finely embroidered rituals might well be what the late American sociologist, Howard Becker, called a "normative reaction to normlessness." This reaction occurs, according to Becker, when one urban sector of society too brusquely invades another, more rural sector,[5] exactly what has happened to the rural farm wives in urban Merrill Court. Merrill Court is a strange mixture of old and new, of a vanishing Oakie culture and a new blue-collar life style, of rural ways in urban settings, of small-town community in mass society, of people oriented toward the young in an age-separated subculture. These internal immigrants to the working-class neighborhoods of West Coast cities and suburbs indeed perceived their new environment through rural and small-town eyes. For example, one woman who had been dress shopping at a department store observed "all those lovely dresses, all stacked like cordwood." * Another habitually said, "What d'ya think of them apples?" as a way of saying "What do you think of that?" A favorite saying when one was about to retire was, "Guess I'll go to bed with the chickens tonight." But the farm life they had known was nowhere in sight. They would give directions to the new hamburger joint or hobby shop by describing its relationship to a small stream or big tree. What remained of the old custom of a funeral wake took place at a new funeral parlor with neon signs and printed notices.

It may be that the communal life in Merrill Court had nothing to do with rural ways in an urban setting. Had the widows stayed on the farms and in the small towns they came from, they might have been active in community life there. I do not know. I do know that those who had been involved in community life before remained active, and with the exception of a few mentioned earlier, those who previously had not, became active.

For whatever reason, the widows built themselves an order out of ambiguity, a set of obligations to the outside and to one another where few had existed before. Perhaps this result could be described in Herbert Marcuse's terms** as "surplus repression." It is possible to relax in old age, to consider one's social debts paid, and to feel that constraints that do not weigh on the far side of the grave should not weigh on the near side either. But in Merrill Court, the watchfulness of social life, the Protestant stress on industry, thrift, and activity added up to an ethos of keeping one's "boots on," not simply as individuals but as a community.

---

* Another warned me to come early to the Christmas party they were having, "because it gets dark awful early these days," even though the party was to be held indoors.
** (See Marcuse, 1955.) One might also interpret this pattern as "escape from freedom." (See Fromm, 1941.)

Social Patterns

The social arrangements that took root early in the history of Merrill Court later assumed a life of their own. They were designed, as if on purpose, to assure an *on-going* community. If we were to visually diagram the community, it would look like a social circle on which there are centripedal and centrifugal pressures. The formal role system, centered in the circle, pulled people toward it by giving them work and rewards, and this process went on mainly "downstairs." At the same time, informal loyalty networks fluctuated toward and away from the circle. They became clear mainly "upstairs." Relatives and outsiders pulled the individual away from the circle downstairs and network upstairs although they were occasionally pulled inside both. We will look at the social arrangements both "downstairs" and "upstairs."

Downstairs: The Biography of a Formal Role

A minor but interesting role "downstairs" was the Secret Pal chairmanship, which in 1967 was filled by a shy, thin woman named Rubie. I shall describe this role to show what it did both for Rubie and for the community. This role, like others, changed hands the Monday after New Year's. After calling for a round of applause for the outgoing chairman, the Recreation Director asked for volunteers. Several tentatively suggested someone else, and Rubie, the first to respond to being nominated, with laughter and side-talk to a neighbor, was declared the Secret Pal Chairman for the year.

She was to see that everyone received a small gift worth no more than $2.00 each Christmas and birthday. Since the gifts were anonymous (given by a secret pal), every anonymous donor had to know the recipient's birthday and what he or she would

like in the way of a $2.00 gift. Rubie inherited from her prede-
cessor a roster of names that she updated. People knew whom
they gave gifts to, but not whom they received them from, and
the Secret Pal Chairman thus manipulated a network of secrets
that she gave out selectively. She worked "behind the scenes"
and her roster was a point of much joking: "What you got on that
list there? Make sure I get somethin' nice."

The arrangement itself resembled the incest taboo in pro-
hibiting emotional alliances between particular pairs of people
and inhibiting rivalry. It was an emotional insurance policy,
distributing the feeling of "being remembered" evenly throughout the group. It also replaced the family, or tried to, in those
cases when a grandmother was forgotten on her birthday.

The work was seasonal. Just before Christmas those who had
forgotten asked Rubie who their secret pal was and what she
wanted for Christmas. One conscientious former chairman kept
an inventory of what each resident received the preceding Christmas and what she wanted the next. As each gift was received,
Rubie was called and received part of the credit; or if a birthday
went by without a gift being received, part of the blame. There
was some dispute about how much responsibility Rubie bore for
a forgetful donor. She received many telephone calls and visits
from donors and recipients alike, and, in this way, the job en-
meshed her in a social network.

Rubie's role was mainly important within Merrill Court,
where she was applauded after presents were distributed; outside
it, the status was not transferable. Most widows had to explain
to uninitiated relatives precisely what a Secret Pal Chairman was
and did.* Ironically, when insiders went outside, the role
diminished in importance; but when outsiders came inside, it
shone forth. When, for example, the mayor and head of the
Recreation Department attended the Christmas Party, there was

---

* A work role, even if others do not know precisely what it involves, is
transferable outside the work context, and even more transferable is
the money that results. Roles in voluntary organizations seldom have
that legitimacy outside the organization.

a round of speeches praising the industry and dedication of club officers. Outside the subculture, the women were pensioners without major functions in life, and to step outside the subculture was to step down socially, or at least to withdraw from a source of social rewards. This situation might account for the fact that even those with low status inside the community (for example, Beatrice the piano player) preferred to remain stigmatized within rather than to become nothing outside.

The role of Secret Pal Chairman never lasted more than a year, and most roles lasted the three months from one banquet to another.* Or rather, the roles lived on but their occupants retired after three months. Hence, responsibility and involvement were widely distributed and new work was always coming up. Over a period of three years, of the six deaths in the building, four of the deceased had jobs, which immediately became available. When Emma returned from the hospital after a minor heart attack, she was offered a role just vacated. The system of offices seemed designed to deal with a "transient" population; if informal friendships were lost through the death of one Secret Pal Chairman, the Secret Pal chairman*ship* lived on impervious.[6]

Upstairs: The Informal Social Web

Shadowing the formal circle was an informal network of friendships that formed over a cup of coffee in the upstairs apartments. The physical appearance of the apartments told something about the network. Inside, each apartment had a living room, kitchen, bedroom, and porch. The apartments were unfurnished when the women moved in and as one remarked, "We fixed 'em up just the way we wanted. I got this new lamp over to Sears, and my daughter and I bought these new scatter rugs. Felt just like a new bride."

For the most part, the apartments were furnished in a re-

---

* Exceptions were the presidency, secretaryship, and treasurership.

markably similar way. Many had American flag stickers outside their doors. Inside, each had a large couch with a floral design, which sometimes doubled as a hide-a-bed where a grandchild might sleep for a weekend. Often a chair, a clock, or picture came from the old home and provided a material link to the past. Most had large stuffed chairs, bowls of homemade artificial flowers, a Bible, and porcelain knickknacks neatly arranged on a table. (When the group was invited to my own apartment for tea, one woman suggested sympathetically that we "had not quite moved in yet" because the apartment seemed bare by comparison.) By the window were potted plants, often grown from a neighbor's slip. A plant might be identified as "Abbie's ivy" or "Ernestine's African violet."

The apartments were so alike to me (although not to the residents) that I was reminded of Leo Tolstoi's short story, "The Death of Ivan Ilych," in which Ivan found and decorated a house just as he himself had fantasized an ideal house, room by room. Although Ivan considered the house an expression of his individuality, it exactly resembled the houses of others in the same social class, with the same aspirations and taste.

There were photographs, usually out of date, of children and grandchildren, and Woolworth pictures of pinkcheeked children on the walls.* Less frequently there was a photo of a deceased husband and less frequently still, a photo of a parent. On the living room table or nearby there was usually a photograph album containing pictures of relatives and pictures of the woman herself on a recent visit "back east." Many of the photographs in the album were arranged in the same way. Pictures of children came first and, of those, children with the most children appeared first, and childless children at the end.

The refrigerator almost always told a social story. One con-

---

* Their preference in art objects was for what Marshall McLuhan calls "hot media." That is, what they liked was realistic, spelled out, unambiguous. They seemed to like flat visual designs rather than sculptural art or paintings with a sculptural dimension. They also liked intricate small objects rather than simple or large objects.

tained homemade butter made by the cousin of a woman on the second floor; berry jam made by the woman three doors down; corn bought downstairs in the Recreation Room, brought in by someone's son who worked in a corn-canning factory; homemade Swedish rolls to be given to a daughter when she came to visit; two dozen eggs to be used in cooking, most of which would be given away; as well as bread and fruit, more than enough for one person. Most of the women had once cooked for large families, and Emma, who raised eight children back in Oklahoma, habitually baked about eight times as much corn bread as she could eat. She made the rounds of apartments on her floor distributing the extra bread. The others who also cooked in quantities reciprocated, also gratuitously, with other kinds of food. It was an informal division of labor although no one thought of it that way.

Most neighbors were also friends and friendships, as well as information about them, were mainly confined to each floor. For example, according to Ernestine, "There was a lot of to-do when Mr. Hill decided to remarry. They say Irma (whom he did not marry) was really, you know, disappointed. But now I don't know. I don't live on that floor."

All but four had their *best* friends on the same floor and only a few had a next-best friend on another floor. The more one had friends outside the building, the more one had friends on *other* floors within the building. That is, the wider one's social radius outside the building, the wider it was inside the building as well.

There was a distinction between socializing over a cup of coffee and socializing over a meal. As Irma commented, "Sometimes I see Rosy in the elevator and she says, 'Come on over for a cup of coffee' or else she calls and I shuffle over in my housecoat and slippers." But she added, "There's a problem, when you invite a person to lunch, you can't know where to stop." Potential guests were not hurt not to be invited for a cup of coffee, but meals were a different matter.

Apart from the gratification of friendship, neighboring did a number of things for the community. It was a way of relaying information or misinformation about others. Often the information relayed upstairs influenced social arrangements downstairs. For example, according to one widow,

> The Bitfords had a tiff with Irma upstairs here, and a lot of tales went around. They weren't true, not a one, about Irma, but then people didn't come downstairs as much. Mattie used to come down, and Marie and Mr. Ball and they don't so much now, only once and again, because of Irma being there. All on account of that tiff.

Often people seated themselves downstairs as they were situated upstairs, neighbor and friend next to neighbor and friend, and a disagreement upstairs filtered downstairs. For example, when opinion was divided and feelings ran high on the issue of whether to store the Club's $900 in a cigar box under the Treasurer's bed or in the bank, the gossip, formerly confined to upstairs invaded the public arena downstairs.

Relaying information this way meant that without directly asking, people knew a lot about one another. It was safe to assume that what you did was known about by at least one network of neighbors and their friends. Even the one social isolate on the third floor, Velma, was known about, and her comings and goings were talked about and judged. Talk about other people was a means of social control and it operated, as it does elsewhere through parables; what was told of another was a message to one's self.

Not all social control was verbal. As I mentioned before, since all apartment living rooms faced out on a common walkway that led to a central elevator, each tenant was usually seen coming and going; and by how he or she was dressed, one could accurately guess what they were about. Since each resident knew the visiting habits of her neighbor, anything unusual was immediately spotted. One day when I was knocking on the door of a resident, her neighbor came out:

> I don't know where she is, it couldn't be the doctor's, she goes to the doctor's on Tuesdays; it couldn't be shopping, she shopped

yesterday with her daughter. I don't think she's downstairs, she says she's worked enough today. Maybe she's visiting Abbie. They neighbor a lot. Try the second floor.

Neighboring is also a way to detect sickness or death. As Ernestine related, "This morning I looked to see if Judson's curtains were open. That's how we do on this floor, when we get up we open our curtains just a bit, so others walking by outside know that everything's all right. And if the curtains aren't drawn by mid-morning, we knock to see." * Mattie perpetually refused to open her curtains in the morning and kept them close to the wall by placing potted plants against them so that "a man won't get in." This excluded her from the checking up system and disconcerted the other residents.

The widows in good health took it upon themselves to care for one or two in poor health. Delia saw after Grandma Goodman who was not well enough to go down and get her mail and shop and Ernestine helped Little Floyd and Mrs. Blackwell who were too blind to cook their own meals. Irma took care of Mr. Cooper and it was she who called his son when Mr. Cooper "took sick." Even those who had not adopted someone to help often looked after a neighbor's potted plants while they were visiting kin, lent kitchen utensils, and took phone messages. One woman wrote letters for those who "wrote a poor hand." **

Some of the caretaking was reciprocal, but most was not. Three people helped to take care of Little Floyd, but since he was blind he could do little in return. Delia fixed his meals, Ernestine laundered his clothes, and Irma shopped for his food.

---

* The function of "keeping an eye out" is more impersonally handled when a peer community is absent. For example, the *St. Petersburg Times* (Florida, August 9, 1969), noted ". . . homebound older persons living alone here, either permanently or temporarily, are eligible for a free "Reassurance Telephone Program." It is offered by the Senior Citizens Referral and Guidance Center. . . . Volunteers call individuals seven days a week (about 5 calls a day) to be sure they're okay, between 9:30 A.M.–3:30 P.M." (Also see Clark and Anderson, 1967.)
** The average had six years of school, but some had not passed the third grade.

When Little Floyd died fairly suddenly, he was missed perhaps more than others who died during those three years, especially by his caretakers. Ernestine remarked sadly, "I liked helping out the poor old fella. He would appreciate the tiniest thing. And never a complaint."

Sometimes people paid one another for favors. For example, Freda took in sewing for a small sum. When she was paid for lining a coat, she normally mentioned the purpose for which the money would be spent (e.g., bus fare for a visit to relatives in Montana), perhaps to reduce the commercial aspect of the exchange. Delia was paid by the Housing Authority for cleaning and cooking for Grandma Goodman, a disabled woman on her floor; and as she repeatedly mentioned to Grandma Goodman, she spent the money on high school class rings for her three grandchildren. In one case, the Housing Authority paid a granddaughter for helping her grandmother with housework. In another case, a disabled woman paid for domestic help from her social security checks.*

Elite and Masses

Downstairs and up, the residents' relations had a comradely side-by-side quality, expressed in the names they called one another. Downstairs people went by last names: Judson, Whitcock, Farmer, Raymond, reminiscent of a roll call in the shipyards. To her relatives Bernice Judson was Bernice and to outsiders, Mrs. Jud-

---

* Among neighbors there was an informal code of etiquette about borrowing money. It was understood that an individual never refused to lend money, but if she didn't want to lend it, she gave a more acceptable reason, such as not having money on hand. In one instance, a neighbor called Delia to borrow three dollars for a taxicab. Delia did not have three dollars, but she borrowed three dollars (from me) to lend to the neighbor. As she explained, "If I said I didn't have the money, she'd have thought I didn't *want* to lend it to her. I didn't want her to think that." Delia borrowed money to lend in order to avoid having her behavior misinterpreted as accepted subterfuge.

son; but downstairs it was "Hey, Judson, come here." Only those on the margins of communal life were called by their formal names. For example, Mr. Cooper, who was defined as slightly senile and was treated as a non-person, was called "Mr. Cooper" never plain "Cooper." Others had pet names; for example, "Grandma Goodman." The 70-year-old blind man called "Little Floyd" was no younger or smaller than any other resident.

Like sisters, their relations were tinged with as much rivalry as friendly support. The rivalry took several forms. In the eyes of the outside world, all at Merrill Court were social equals, but within the community there was an elite, a counter-elite, and the masses. What were coexisting friendship networks in time of peace became rivaling juntas when an issue arose. Although there were many separate friendship duos and trios, nearly all of them sided with either the elite or the counter-elite. It was perhaps no accident that the two groups were divided by region, the first including people from Virginia, Oklahoma, and Tennessee, the second, from Wisconsin and Montana. The two cliques also worshipped at different Baptist churches.

How an issue divided the group depended on the whereabouts of gossip or "meta-gossip" (talk about gossip). In this "meta-gossip," malicious or unkind words were not in themselves forbidden or worried about, only unkind words spoken in public. On one occasion some unkind words were spoken downstairs, and people began to trouble over "the gossip problem." The very same unkind words had been spoken upstairs, in my presence, and had not been defined as "a problem" then.

According to each junta, the other was a source of "bad tales." * The leader of the counter-elite was Mrs. Farmer. As

---

* Gossip seemed to be a constant threat to public occasions, barred from them only by the fear of reprisal. That fear may be an important dimension of what we mean by social solidarity. In the case mentioned above, a widow had commented, "Due to feeling so poorly I'm resigning from the birthday chairmanship. There are those who say I haven't been doing a good job. . . ." Others responded to the accusation and a crisis arose. The comment itself seemed harmless enough, except insofar as it publicly accused some gossipers.

Treasurer for three years running, she was the Talleyrand of the community's political life. Other officeholders would come and go but Mrs. Farmer was always Treasurer. She was also a main source of disaffection and as the stratum of "underdogs" (non-officeholders) changed, so would the membership of the junta centered around her. She apparently started the "rumor" that a woman was taking trips to Reno to deposit extra money in a bank there in order to avoid exceeding the maximum income to qualify for welfare. The elite, figuring that the woman in question had been on A.D.C. for twelve years, decided that the rumor was false and so accused the rumor-spreaders. The same happened to a rumor about another member who was said to have smuggled in an expensive sewing machine that might have disqualified her for welfare. The same information or misinformation ran both circuits but what was fact to one was rumor to the other. It did seem that the counter-elite, which had only one officeholder and was thus more socially on the bottom, was the source of more rumors. The elite, composed entirely of club officers, seemed to spend more time squelching rumors. However, my own association with the elite junta may have biased my observations.

The elite more often stressed "service to others" whereas the masses were more isolationist, stressing rewards "at home." Delia, who like past club presidents, came from a small town, summed up the situation from her viewpoint:

Since I've become president here, I feel we are part of Verada just like the VFW and the Eagles. "Why do they come to us [referring to other organizations]?" some of the women ask. They come and say we want 50 favors to be made for the Mayor's conference. They come to us because they think we can do the job; they wouldn't come to us if they didn't think that. It's an honor. But so many here feel we shouldn't have any truck with that. They don't want our mad money used on anyone else. They don't want to pay $40 for a self-portrait of Reena [the Recreation Director who fell ill]. They don't want to have to pay for a dinner to honor her. What has she done for us? they ask. If I tell them all the contribution she made to the com-

56

munity outside of us, they think she shouldn't be rewarded for that, only for what she's done for us. They're always wanting a special dinner price for relatives. They don't care beans about what we can do for others. You might call it selfish.

On the other hand, the out-group complained that Delia and her henchmen were "hobnobbing" with those people in the Recreation Department, and being exploited by them. "We work and she gets the credit. Is that any way to run a ship?" The pattern persisted in the face of three turnovers in leadership, so that the three succeeding club presidents came, in turn, to espouse the "contribution" view while the masses tended more to the "rewards at home" view.

Both the "foreign aid" and the "isolationist" policies seemed to be linked to the distribution of rewards for aid offered outside organizations. Delia was directly rewarded on *behalf* of Merrill Court; the isolationists symbolically rewarded only *through* their leader. When the club did a good turn for the Cancer Society or the boys in Vietnam, thank-you letters were addressed back to the club President. It was the President and the two officers next in line who were invited to visit a "beautification" program, or to lunch with other presidents of voluntary organizations such as the Garden Club, the Daughters of Rebecca, and the Hillcrest Junior Women's Club. On one occasion the President and her officers were invited by the Recreation and Parks Department to view a cemetery on which trees were sold for $3 each. The President, Delia, bought a tree not for the club but for herself in memory of her deceased husband. The counter-elite and the masses, who had not been invited, began finding fault with Delia and complaining about "thankless chores" shortly thereafter.

The masses more often mentioned the fact of age, which democratized the group. For example, as Mrs. Farmer frequently brought out, "We're all elder people here. The club President isn't a day younger than any of us. There's no reason for her to be feeling so special." On the other hand, the ruling elite, *while* it was that, seldom mentioned age. They equated themselves, rather, with the Veterans of Foreign Wars and the Lions Club, whose memberships are not based on age.* Outside of Merrill Court, the residents were all "the senior citizens over at the project," and there was no distinguishing between the masses and their representatives.

The "Poor Dear" Hierarchy

Parallel to the distinction between elite and masses was an informal status hierarchy that had little to do with the formal social circle. If within the formal social circle there was a status hierarchy based on the distribution of *honor,* there also was a parallel hierarchy based on the distribution of luck. In fact, "luck" is not entirely luck. Health and life expectancy, for example, are often considered "luck," ** but an upper-class person can expect to live ten years longer than a lower-class person. The widows of Merrill Court, however, were drawn from the same social class and they saw the differences among themselves as matters of luck.

There was a shared system of ranking according to which she who had good health won honor. She who lost the fewest loved ones through death won honor and she who was close to her children won honor. Those who fell short on any of these criteria were often referred to as "poor dears."

The "poor dear" system operated like a set of valves through

---

* Age was also occasionally invoked as an explanation for disharmony. For example, when there had been a series of feuds concerning the annual bazaar, the women informally diagnosed the situation; "We're none of us getting any younger. Some of us can't work as well as before. Last year we had Alma with us. She was a real worker." However, a month later when the issue had been resolved, age was never mentioned, nor were the deaths that had occurred since the last bazaar.
** Even the number of children one has, and one's relation to them, are not entirely matters of "luck." For a short story that touches on this general question, see J. F. Powers, "The Poor Thing," in *The Presence of Grace* (1956). For a study of the relationship between social class and life expectancy, see Mayer and Hauser (1953).

which a sense of superiority ran in only one direction. Someone who was a "poor dear" in the eyes of another seldom called that other person a "poor dear" in return; but seldom did anyone accept the label from "above." Rather, the "poor dear" would turn to someone felt to be less fortunate, perhaps to buttress a sense of her own achieved or ascribed superiority.* Thus, the hierarchy honored residents at the top and pitied "poor dears" at the bottom, creating a number of informally recognized status distinctions among those who, in the eyes of the outside society, were social equals.

It is a tricky business to link feelings, which psychologists mainly deal with, with social distinctions, which mainly concern sociologists, but I offer the following. How one fares in the distribution of luck can be compared to how one fares in the distribution of "earned" honor. In both cases, the unequal distribution has to be socially handled. How one fares in the distribution of luck has by definition nothing to do with merit. One cannot help it if one's husband dies or one has a heart attack. But luck, once it *has* been unequally distributed, and becomes ascribed, is also socially handled much as the earned honor is socially handled.

In both cases, the haves experience different emotions toward the have-nots than the have-nots experience toward the haves. The haves of fate often experience pity or its negative companion, scorn, for the have-nots. And the have-nots, in turn, feel envy for the haves. In the distribution of honor, on the other hand, the haves feel charity looking down, and the unhonored feel respect, which includes an element of fear, looking up.** Perhaps the have-nots of respect feel envy like the have-nots of fate, but envy in the first case is less legitimate since there is the

* One does not always respect those one fears, but I suggest there is almost always an element of (legitimated) fear in respect.
** The respected person is free to protect himself from social encounters by invoking the fear in others that is his due. On the other hand, he is also free to undo the fear, and reduce social distance. The non-respected have no such choice.

ideological cushion that respect is earned, whereas luck is not. If one has not earned respect, it is thought to be one's own fault. Insofar as luck is concerned, envy is more readily and legitimately felt since there seems to be no justice in the distribution of luck. As regards both luck and respect, those feelings probably exist only in relation to those to whom one is, in *other* respects, socially equal and thus comparable. In both cases there is social distance between the respected and unrespected, lucky and unlucky. Although the unlucky do not blame themselves for bad luck, and do not accept a stigmatized status, the lucky impose it on them, especially the *relatively* lucky. The unlucky (or pitied), perhaps to avoid the unpleasant emotion of envy, turn to others whom they themselves can pity. In behavioral terms, the unlucky receive solicitous behavior from above, ward it off, and in turn are solicitous toward others still less fortunate.

The distinctions made by residents of Merrill Court are only part of a larger old age status hierarchy based on things other than luck. At the monthly meetings of the countywide Senior Citizens Forum, to which Merrill Court sent two representatives, the term "poor dear" often arose with reference to old people. It was "we senior citizens who are politically involved versus those 'poor dears' who are active in recreation." Those active in recreation, however, did not accept a subordinate position relative to the politically active. On the other hand, they did not refer to the political activists as "poor dears." Within the politically active group there were those who espoused general causes, such as getting out an anti-pollution bill, and those who espoused causes related only to old age, such as raising social security benefits or improving medical benefits. Those in politics and recreation referred to the passive card players and newspaper readers as "poor dears." Old people with passive life styles in good health referred to those in poor health as "poor dears" and those in poor health but living in independent housing referred to those in nursing homes as "poor dears." Within the nursing home there was a distinction between those who were ambulatory and those who were not. Among those who were not ambulatory there was a distinction between those who could enjoy food and those who could not. Almost everyone, it seemed, had a "poor dear."

At Merrill Court, the main distinction was between people like themselves and people in nursing homes. Returning from one of the monthly trips to a nearby nursing home, one resident commented:

> There was an old woman in a wheel chair there with a dolly in her arms. I leaned over to look at the dolly. I didn't touch it, well, maybe I just brushed it. She snatched it away, and said "Don't take my dolly." They're pathetic, some of them, the poor dears.

Another woman, a 69-year-old widow, noted:

> I like to talk to old people (referring to a 105-year-old woman in a nursing home). It's not boring. They have a lot of interesting things to say. I talk to them and every so often I break in, you know. But mostly I just let her talk. She likes to have someone to tell things to.[7]

Even within the building, those who were in poor health, were alienated from their children, or were aging rapidly were considered "poor dears." It was lucky to be young and unlucky to be old. There was more than a twenty-year age span between the youngest and oldest in the community. When one of the younger women, Delia, age 69, was drinking coffee with Grandma Goodman, age 79, they compared ages. It was Grandma Goodman who dwelt on the subject and finished the conversation by citing the case of Mrs. Blackwell, who was 89 and still in reasonably good health. Another remarked about her 70th birthday:

> I just couldn't imagine myself being 70. Seventy is old! That's what Daisy said too. She's 80 you know. It was her 70th that got her. No one likes to be put aside, you know. Laid away. Put on the shelf you might say. No sir.

She had an ailment that prevented her from bowling or lifting her flower pots, but she compared her health to that of Daisy, and found her own health a source of luck.

Old people compare themselves not to the young but to other old people. Often the residents referred to the old back in Oklahoma, Texas, and Arkansas with pity in their voices:

> Back in Oklahoma, why they toss the old people away like old shoes. My old friends was all livin' together in one part of town and they hardly budged the whole day. Just sat out on their porch and chewed the fat. Sometimes they didn't even do that. Mostly they didn't have no nice housing, and nothin' social was goin' on. People here don't know what luck they've fallen into.

They also compared their lot to that of other older people in the area. As one resident said:

> Some of my friends live in La Casa [another housing project]. I suppose because they have to, you know. And I tried to get them to come bowling with me, but they wouldn't have a thing to do with it. "Those senior citizens, that's old folks stuff." Wouldn't have a thing to do with it. I tried to tell them we was pretty spry, but they wouldn't listen. They just go their own way. They don't think we have fun.

On the whole, the widows disassociated themselves from the status of "old person," and accepted its "minority" characteristics.[8] The "poor dears" in the nursing home were often referred to as childlike: "They are easily hurt, you know. They get upset at the slightest thing and they like things to be the way they've always been. Just like kids." Occasionally, a widow would talk about Merrill Court itself in this vein, presumably excluding herself: "We're just like a bunch of kids here sometimes. All the sparring that goes on, even with church folk. And people get so hurt, so touchy. You'd think we were babies sometimes."

If the widows accepted the stereotypes of old age, they did not add the "poor dear" when referring to themselves. But younger outsiders did. To the junior employees in the Recreation and Parks Department, the young doctors who treated them at the county hospital, the middle-aged welfare workers, and the young bank tellers, the residents of Merrill Court, and old people like them, were "poor dears."

Perhaps in old age there is a premium on finishing life off with the feeling of being a "have." * But during old age, one also occupies a low social position. The way the old look for luck differences among themselves reflects the pattern found at the bottom of other social, racial, and gender hierarchies. To find oneself lucky within an ill-fated category is to gain the semblance of high status when society withholds it from others in the category. The way in which old people feel above and condescend to other old people may be linked to the fact that the young feel above and condescend to them. The luck hierarchy does not stop with the old.[9]

The Sibling Bond

Rivalries and differences there were in Merrill Court but not alienation and not isolation. A club member who stayed up in her apartment during club meetings more often did it out of spite than indifference. More obvious were the many small, quiet favors, keeping an eye out for a friend and sharing a good laugh.

There was something special about this community, not so much because it was an old age subculture, but because the subculture was founded on a particular kind of *relationship,* the sibling bond. In what follows I will describe the sibling bond, show how it appeared in Merrill Court, and then discuss the link between the sibling bond and social trends. The link is briefly the following: 1) the faster the rate of social change, the more society is stratified by age; 2) the more it is stratified by age, the larger the pool of potential social siblings; 3) such pools,

---

* This comes close to what Erik Erikson calls a sense of integrity, which wins over a sense of despair in the successful resolution of the final life crisis. (Erikson, 1959).

as pointed out in Chapter Two, can sometimes coalesce into peer communities such as this. However, this happens only under certain conditions, as relations between old people in nursing homes and in hospital wards show.

There are two basic types of relations* and all bonds in some way resemble one or the other: the parent-child and the sibling bonds.[10] These are what German sociologist Max Weber called "ideal types" or abstract models against which one can compare every day, real relationships. They do not necessarily refer to relations between *actual* siblings or *actual* parents and children. Actual siblings are likely to have a "sibling bond" but they may not, just as actual parents and children may not, have a "parent-child bond." The sibling bond involves 1) reciprocity, and 2) similarity between two people.[11] Reciprocity implies equality; what you do for me I return to you in equal measure. We can depend on each other a lot or a little but we depend on and give to each other equally. If the exchange is not always even, the feeling is that it should be. The sibling bond also involves similarity between people: I have the same things to offer and the same needs to fill that you have. On one hand, this relationship opens up the potential for community based on similar interests, and on the other hand, feeds the potential for rivalry based on the competition to fulfill similar needs. Like the relationship between real siblings, it can reflect feelings (hostility, for example) that have their roots in another (parent-child) relationship.

By contrast, the parent-child bond is not based on reciprocity

---

* Any relationship has many more dimensions than I am talking about here; for example, the extent to which it is intimate or impersonal, based on one specific thing in common or many things in common. I am focusing here on two dimensions—complementarity and reciprocity.

Since there are two dimensions, we have four theoretically possible combinations: 1) complementary and reciprocal (e.g., Grandma Goodman who pays Delia to do work for her), 2) complementary and non-reciprocal (e.g., Mr. Cooper who needs help but can't return the favor), 3) similar and reciprocal (most relations in Merrill Court), and 4) similar and non-reciprocal (two people who need the same service, though only one can give it).

or similarity. What you do for me I cannot return in equal measure. I depend on you more than you depend on me. And what is exchanged is different, not similar. Very old people often need care and their mature children may have a (not quite commensurate) need to nurture. In the parent-child bond, there are fewer similar needs, resources, or experiences and more different resources exchanged, different needs met, and different experiences shared.

Speaking about the relations of real parents to children, and brothers to sisters, Freud wrote: "We find an absence of love far more repellent between parent and child than between brothers and sisters. In the former case we have, as it were, made something sacred which in the latter we have left profane." [12] Freud discusses social substitutes for this profane sibling relation in his *Group Psychology and the Analysis of the Ego.* Each follower in a group has a parent-child relation with the leader but a sibling bond to his fellow followers. This brotherhood of followers is governed by the rule of justice and equality. As Freud put it, "No one must want to put himself forward; everyone must be the same and have the same." [13]

The sacred and more indispensable parent-child bond fills complementary needs and binds polarities. The profane sibling bond provides a fellowship to shore up one end of the complementary relationship, often reducing aloneness in a different way, with laughter more than comfort, conviviality more than the act of being needed. The sibling bond seeks for other "me's" rather than "you's." In psychological terms, in the sibling relationship, one identifies with the other sibling more but takes that other sibling as an "object" less.

Most residents of Merrill Court are social siblings. The custom of exchanging cups of coffee, lunches, potted plants, and curtain checking suggest reciprocity. Upstairs, one widow usually visited as much as she was visited. In deciding who visits whom, they often remarked, "Well, I came over last time. You come over this time." They traded, in even measure, slips from house plants, kitchen utensils, and food of all sorts. They watched one another's apartments when someone was away on a visit, and they called and took calls for one another.

There are hints of the parent-child bond in the *protégé* system, but protectors picked their protégés voluntarily and resented taking care of people they did not volunteer to help. For example, one protector of "Little Floyd" complained about a crippled club member, a non-resident:

> It wasn't considerate of Rose to expect us to take care of her. She can't climb in and out of the bus very well and she walks so slow. The rest of us wanted to see the museum. It's not nice to say, but I didn't want to miss the museum waiting for her to walk with us. Why doesn't her son take her on trips?

The quality of a relation was reflected in their telephoning voices. I began to notice that when they answered the phone, as I was sitting in their apartments, I could predict the category of the person at the other end of the line. Their tone of voice was soft and receptive and they listened longer when it was a child. It was louder, gayer, and there was more talk interspersed with listening when it was a peer. Also, the content of the talk was different. With relatives, they might ask after relatives, or a granddaughter might ask what to do after the rolls in the oven have risen once. With peers it was more likely to be a comment such as "What are you wearing tonight?" or "Wasn't that something about Rose and the museum?" or a comment explaining the outcome of a visit to the doctor. The comments with relatives involved a dissimilarity of experience, those with peers a similarity.

The widows were not only equals among themselves, they also were remarkably similar. They all wanted more or less the same things and could give more or less the same things. They all wanted to *receive* Mother's Day cards. No one in the building *sent* Mother's Day cards. And what they did was to *compare* Mother's Day cards. Although there was some division of labor, there was little difference in labor performed. All knew how to bake bread and can peaches, but no one knew how to fix faucets. They all knew about "the old days" but few among them could explain what was going on with youth these days. They all had ailments but no one there could cure them. They all needed rides to the shopping center, but no one among them needed riders. There was little of the complementarity that goes with the parent-child relation.

Their similar functions meant that when they did exchange services, it was usually the same kinds of services they themselves could perform. For example, two neighbors might exchange corn bread for jam, but both knew how to make both corn bread *and* jam. If one neighbor made corn bread for five people in one day, one of the recipients would also make corn bread for the same people two weeks later. Each specialized within a specialization, and over the long run the widows made and exchanged the same goods.

Hence the "side by sideness," the "in the same boat" quality of their relations. They noticed the same things about the world and their eyes caught the same items in a department store. They noticed the same features in the urban landscape—the pastor's home, the Baptist church, the nursing homes, the funeral parlors, the places that used to be. They did not notice, as an adolescent might, the gas stations and hamburger joints.

As a result, they were good listeners to one another. It was common for someone to walk into the Recreation Room and launch into the details of the latest episode of a mid-afternoon television drama ("It seems that the baby is not by artificial insemination but really Frank's child, and the doctor is trying to convince her to tell. . . ."). The speaker could safely assume that her listeners also knew the details. Since they shared many experiences, a physical ailment, a death, a description of the past, an "old age joke" could be explained, understood, and enjoyed. They talked together about their children much as their children, together, talked about them. Each shared with social siblings one side of a parent-child bond.

This similarity opened up the possibility of comparison and

rivalry,* as the "poor dear" hierarchy suggests. In the same way, distinctions between the "elite" and "masses" were based on the assumption that people were similar and that everyone was equal to start with. Whether the widows cooperated in collecting money for flowers, or competed for prestigious offices in the Service Club, bowling trophies, or front seats in the bus, their functions were similar, their status roughly equal, and their relations in the best and worst sense, "profane."

Not all groups of old people form this sibling bond—for example, old people in institutions do not. All things being equal, we might expect subcultures to also arise in nursing homes, certain hospital wards, or convalescent hospitals. To begin with, all things are not equal; the institutionalized tend to be older, physically weaker, poorer, and initially more isolated than their peers in the population at large.[14]

But even among the fairly healthy and ambulatory within institutions, the likes of Merrill Court is rare. It is not enough to put fairly healthy, socially similar old people together. There is clearly something different between institutions and public housing apartments. Perhaps what counts is the kind of relationships that institutions foster. The resident of an institution is "a patient." Like a child, he has his meals served to him, his water glass filled, his bed made, his blinds adjusted by the "mother-nurse." He cannot return the service. Although he often shares a room or a floor with "brother" patients, both siblings have a non-reciprocal relationship to attendants or nurses. Even the research on the institutionalized focuses on the relation between patient and attendant, not between patient and patient. If there is a strong parent-child bond, it may overwhelm any potential

---

* There is the notion that comparisons between people are only "fair" when a number of factors are held constant. A parent may not compare his own performance with that of his child because the comparison is "unfair." They differ in too many ways to make the comparison meaningful. When a widow says of another, "She is doing well," she means "She is doing well for a 69-year-old lower-class white widow."

sibling solidarity. If the old in institutions meet as equals, it is not as independent equals. The patient's relation to other patients is like the relation between *real*, young siblings, which may exaggerate rather than forestall narcissistic withdrawal.

The widows of Merrill Court took care of themselves, fixed their own meals, paid their own rent, shopped for their own food, and made their own beds; and they did these things for others. Their sisterhood rests on adult autonomy. This is what people at Merrill Court have and people in institutions do not.

The Sibling Bond and Age-Stratification

The sibling bond is delicate and emerges only when conditions are ripe. Rapid currents of social change, as Chapter Two suggests, lead to age-stratification, which, in turn, ripens conditions for the sibling bond. Tied to his fellows by sibling bonds, an individual is cemented side by side into an age stratum with which he shares the same rewards, wants, abilities, and failings.

French sociologist Emile Durkheim, in his book *The Division of Labor*, describes two forms of social solidarity.[15] To oversimplify, in organic solidarity there is a division of labor, complementary dependence, and differences among people. In mechanical solidarity there is no division of labor, self-sufficiency, and similarity among people. Modern American society as a whole is based on organic solidarity, not only in the economic but in the social, emotional, and intellectual spheres.

Different *age strata* within the general society however, are more bound by *mechanical* solidarity. This is important both for the individual and the society. Although division of labor, complementary dependence, and differences among people describe society's network of relations as a whole, they do not adequately describe relations among particular individuals. An individual's complementary dependence may be with people he does not know or meet—such as the person who grows and cans the food he eats, or lays the bricks for his house. Again in his most intimate relations, an individual may have complementary relations* (either equal or unequal) with his spouse and children. But in between the most and least intimate bonds is a range in which there are many sibling relationships which form the basis of mechanical solidarity.

In fact, many every-day relations are with people similar and equal to oneself. Relations between colleague and colleague, student and student, girl friend and girl friend, boy friend and boy friend, relations within a wives group, or "the guys at the bar," the teenage gang, the army buddies are often forms of the sibling bond. These ties are often "back up relations," social insurance policies for the times when the complementary bonds of parent and child, husband and wife, student and teacher, boy friend and girl friend fail, falter, or normally change.

From an individual's viewpoint, some periods of life, such as adolescence and old age, are better for forming sibling bonds than are other periods.** Both just before starting a family and after raising one, before entering the economy and after leaving it, an individual is open to, and needs, these back up relationships. It is these stages that are "problematic," and it is these stages that, with longer education and earlier retirement, now last longer. It is in precisely these periods that social siblings are sought.

From society's point of view,[16] the sibling bond allows more flexibility in relations between generations by forging solidarity *within* generations and divisions *between* them. This divides

---

* It may be that rapid social change tends to accent the sibling bond between husband and wife and between parent and child. It has been noted that wife and husband are more equal and more similar (their roles are less differentiated) and more like siblings than husbands and wives used to be a hundred years ago. The parent too is less "parental," and more of a "pal" and companion than an authority.

** Two authors have suggested that organic solidarity prevails in childhood, mechanical solidarity in adolescence, organic solidarity in adulthood, and mechanical once again in old age. At the very end of life there is sometimes a reversal to vertical solidarity similar to that of childhood. (See Cumming and Henry, 1961.)

society into age layers that are relatively more independent of one another, so that changes in one age layer need not be retarded by conditions in another. As suggested in Chapter Two, the institution that has bound the generations together—the family—is in this respect on the decline. As it declines, the sibling bond emerges, filling in and enhancing social flexibility, especially in those social strata where social change is most pronounced. The resulting social flexibility does not guarantee "good" changes and continuity is partly sacrificed to fads and a cult of newness. But whether desirable or not, this flexibility is partly due to and partly causes the growing importance of the sibling bond.

Thus, the times are ripe for the sibling bond, and for old age communities such as Merrill Court. In the social life of old people it is not the sibling bond versus the parent-child bond. Rather, the question is how the one bond complements the other. As Chapter Five shows, the sisterhood at Merrill Court is no substitute for love of children and contact with them; but it offers a full, meaningful life independent of them.

chapter four

WHEN OLD PEOPLE ARE TOGETHER

Grandma: "I suppose I deserve being talked to that way. I've gotten so old. Most people think that when you get so old, you either freeze to death, or you burn up. But you don't. When you get so old, all that happens is that people talk to you that way."

The American Dream, 1961,
by Edward Albee, p. 64

Reprinted by permission of Coward,
McCann & Geoghegan, Inc.

The widows remember similar things, worry about similar problems, and laugh at similar jokes. This likeness might dull their sensibilities and enclose them in a small world, cut off from the young and from people different from themselves. To some extent it did, but what struck me most was the way in which this similarity between widows liberated them and liberated their topics of conversation, especially the topic of death.

In their own company, old people can be in some ways freer.[1] For example, with no young people around, they can dance and sing without fear of seeming "silly." At a typical Merrill Court party, the band, dressed in homemade uniforms, assembles; three with tambourines, one at the broom-and-tub bass, another at the washboard, and one at the piano. The tambourine players look to the audience for encouragement and begin a jig. Some in the audience join in, clapping in time, and before long almost everyone is on the floor dancing around. Even an outsider who comes in in a wheelchair manages a little dance *in situ*. Although two dancers may focus their eyes on each other, it is not a dance of partners but a collective dance. In the eyes of younger people, this is not what grandmothers "do."

On occasions, away from young people, the old are able, as we have seen, to improvise new roles. Just as there is a role of women in sex-integrated company and a role of black in race-integrated company, so there is a role of old person in age-integrated company. One plays woman with men, black with white, and old with young people. To remove whites from the Student Nonviolent Coordinating Committee (SNCC) and men from Women's Liberation groups is to remove the people toward whom blacks and women act a role. In a mixed group of men and women, black and white, old and young, it is the middle-aged white males who generally assume the chairmanships. Blacks and women, in the absence of whites or men, may feel less inhibited in initiating action, giving orders, and assuming authority. It is the same with the old.

To bring old people together is not to free them from all social constraint. Any community stakes out the boundaries of permissibility and stigmatizes the ones, like Beatrice the piano player, who exceed them. But together, the old can establish new and different boundaries. These would not "liberate" them if the larger society did not restrict the sexual, social, and political life of old people, confining them by disapproval or the fear of it.[2]

Old people together not only act but also talk differently from the way they do when they are with young people. This occurred to me only in my third year of participant observation, as I presumably became more of a "non-person." I do not believe the widows thought their conversations together much different from conversations with the young. A *conscious* policy on talk extended only to gossip about residents, politics, and religion. These topics were formally banned from the conversational circuits of the Recreation Room, though they nevertheless habitually came up. When they did, as for example when Southern were compared to American Baptists, someone would puncture the argument: "There are two things we never talk about—religion and politics." * Having established the boundaries of permissibility, the boundaries *themselves* became a topic. These were the only signs that the group explicitly recognized a link between what one talks about and whom one talks with, but these two factors were linked all the time in subtle ways.

One reason for the linkage is that some topics were more interesting or relevant to the old than to their younger families or friends; for example, whether Medicare pays for chiropractors, visiting hours at various hospitals, the merits of various kinds of dentures, yarn prices, the cost of TV repairs, old recipes, and the latest episode in daytime TV serials. When daughters dropped in downstairs, the topic would generally shift to something current of more mutual concern, such as the Edward Kennedy scandal or whether Jackie Kennedy had gone downhill since marrying Onassis.

Apart from these topics were others that came up mainly among old people: talk about the old days and about what it means to grow old and to die. Talk about the old days came up more when the residents were among themselves than when they were with young people; and when it did come up it had a different meaning. When the residents related stories from the past

---

* If the conversation did not move off politics or religion after such a comment there were either 1) general remarks to which most of the group could agree (e.g., "Everybody has his own religion, but it's the same God.") or 2) the person whose intolerance had been exposed would remark about another even less tolerant (e.g., "Bertha thinks that no one goes to heaven who hasn't been baptized. Now I don't believe that."), or, 3) it would turn to a topic related to religion that united the group—such as death.

to young people, it was more to instruct or entertain than to seek confirmation.

When the old people were together alone, everyone was a representative of the past, and no one had to instruct or interpret. They felt free mentally to move back a generation and speak of themselves less as grandmothers and mothers and more as sisters and children of their own deceased parents. They reviewed bits and snatches of memory, one person chiming in after another. This talk seemed to be a way of collectively reviewing the past in order to "feel right" about the way it defined them. According to psychoanalyst Erik Erikson, an individual faces an internal crisis in old age that depends on the resolution of previous crises. An old person who has successfully resolved this crisis has a sense of "integrity," marked by his readiness ". . . to defend the dignity of his own life style against all physical and economic threats" and the knowledge that ". . . for him all human integrity stands and falls with the one style of integrity of which he partakes.[3]

At the same time, the life style, the beliefs and customs on which the old pin their integrity, is now almost nowhere in evidence. Oldness and old fashionedness* are not bound together in every society or in all people; but for the widows of Merrill Court, times have changed as they have aged in a way that perhaps exaggerates the experience of others. For example, Emma Fieldstone was born in 1890 in a covered wagon in western Oklahoma, but now returns there every year on a jet airliner. The old place itself isn't the same. One woman reported after a visit back to Texas, "The old homestead is used for a haybarn now. There were four cars in Emson Valley when I left. Didn't used to be none. It's all highways now." Another returned to a farm that had become a soil bank; a third found new housing tracts built over the old homestead.

These social changes put an additional burden on the crisis

* The old no longer have the power to enforce their opinions and values on others. In fact, the old may be considered "old fashioned" because they lack the power to determine what *is* fashion and what is not.

of integrity. Only in a society that has moved from covered wagons to jet airliners in one lifetime is the old person likely to peg his integrity on, and to defend the dignity of, a vanishing way of life. In this context, integrity can mean endorsing ways of doing things that are no longer generally accepted. The grandmothers watch TV dramas that glamorize divorce and re-entry into the marriage market, whereas in their youth such behavior was frowned upon. They watch their grandchildren graduate from high school and enter junior college when such a thing was almost unheard of in their youth. Their granddaughters are not interested in learning to darn a sock, embroider a pillow case, quilt, or make a rag rug. They have no one to teach how to drip lye, to make soap, to heat the iron on the stove and not burn the clothes, or to skin a rabbit.

Just as the old have no models drawn from previous generations of how to grow old, so too they lack models of how to base integrity on old-fashioned ways, how to incorporate changes without letting the acceptance of new ways jeopardize the integrity of the old ones. Without support from the wider society, this sense of integrity is much easier to achieve in a subculture of old people. Among themselves, the residents felt little need to "defend" their life style, which is everywhere vanishing from contemporary life. On the contrary, many felt sorry for the young because they were missing the "good old days." As one woman put it, "I wouldn't trade lives with nobody. No sir. We worked hard in those days but we had more fun than a pig in the sunshine." The old defenses necessary elsewhere are, in this context, no longer needed. On one occasion in the Recreation Room, after making a mistake in the rug she was weaving, Emma Fieldstone commented, "I guess I'm just a dumb Okie." Another immeditely retorted, "I'm an Oakie too and proud of it. Don't you let me hear you talkin' like that, Emma Fieldstone." The peer community immunizes its members against the full brunt of stigma attached to old ways,*

---

* Initially, I expected the widows to rest their sense of integrity mostly on personal relations that are more immune, presumably, to

and in this case, lower-class, rural ways. At the same time it immunizes society from customs and beliefs that are more short-lived than the people who hold them.*

Even among themselves, the widows did not dwell on the past. There was talk about the past but it was not the thing talked about most. Talk revolved more around last week's excursion and what food to serve at next week's potluck supper than what crops were grown on the farm in their youth. They often talked about the present with categories appropriate to the past. For example, in one telephone conversation, Irma began, "Well, nobody's married, got a new car, or had a baby." After laughing at her remarks, Irma gave a digest of activities in the last four days and a preview of next month's events.

The different sense of relevance that attached to memories and present events reflected itself also in humor. Certain things struck the widows as funny that tended to leave younger people merely smiling politely.** So most joking about old age tended to go on only in the presence of other old people. For example,

---

technological change. This was not the case. For the widows there was no thought that they had wasted time doing things by hand that machines can do now. As one Oklahoma farm wife noted proudly, "I brought up all ma kids on the board," by which she meant that she had washed all her children's clothes on a washboard. The widows feel like a graduate student might feel if told that a dissertation which had taken him four years now results from feeding a computer a problem, specifying a writing style, parameters for data research, and waiting twenty minutes for a 400-page freshly typed manuscript. Such a graduate student might be prone to defend the old way of writing dissertations. He might point out that the computer does not do as good a job, just as the widows say that washing machines do not get clothes as clean these days. One might also be mistaken.

* One might say that the "life span" of norms is getting shorter while the life span of individuals is getting longer.

** If one person laughs, that is one thing; if an entire group laughs simultaneously, it is another. Collective laughter suggests something about shared points of tension and shared experience among the old that is not shared in age-integrated company. Similarly, what becomes an issue and what does not tells something about the nature of the group's solidarity in a way that an attitude or a laugh *taken individually* does not.

one widow entered the Recreation Room wearing a new dress that made her stomach appear to protrude. She was greeted with remarks, "Oh, are you pregnant, Rosy? Didn't know you still had it in you!" Or, "There's life in the old girl yet," or "We haven't been keeping an eye on Judson. You never know what she's been up to!" There were many other jokes concerning pretended pregnancy.

On another occasion, the mailman delivered free toothpaste samples to all the Merrill Court mailboxes. All but one of the residents wear dentures for which ordinary toothpaste is unnecessary. The woman seated in the Recreation Room called out to the mailman, when he had left, "How did you know! Just what we wanted!" and "Good for the mailman, he remembered us on Mother's Day." It was also a standard joke to pretend to offer someone a piece of gum.

A number of the women frequently joked about their wills. For example, when someone brought Jessie a cup of coffee, or picked up something that she had dropped on the floor, she would quip, "Oh, darn, now I gotta go change my will."

They occasionally joked about playing the role of old person. One favorite story a resident told on herself concerned how she tried to get out of jury duty in the county court by confiding to the judge that she was deaf, which she was not. The judge, doubting her somewhat, began to talk more and more softly, asking each time if she could hear him, until she finally replied "just barely." He then dismissed her and she turned her back to go. As she walked away to the door, the judge called out, "Goodbye, Mrs. Riverton." She turned and cheerfully returned the goodbye, showing to all that she could hear perfectly well. On another occasion, a woman refused a job as secretary of the VFW "because of her eyes," although she willingly took the job of treasurer that she liked better. Although she explained the situation seriously, it was received with smiles.

They also discussed the less humorous social and physical aspects of growing old. They agreed, for example, that as old people, they were often treated as part of a category that was not well respected. One woman reported a harrowing encounter with some adolescents:

> I was walking home from shopping. I guess it was Thursday. And there was this young fella, see, and his friend. I was carrying my groceries. They were heavy. And I was walking, you know, kinda slow. And that young fella called out, "Why aren't you in your grave?" He and his friend laughed.

Others brought similar stories before the court of peers. In these stories adolescents were usually the chief villains and they were roundly condemned, although blame often shifted from them to their overly permissive parents. As we have seen, although they were treated as members of a minority group, they themselves talked about old people in the same terms; i.e., as childlike, unable to take responsibility. One common diagnosis for this tendency was summed up by a woman, "They need to be needed. That's the problem. Nobody asks them to do anything. That's why some of them go senile. We don't have that here though." *

Even more serious were their discussions of death. It was a fact of life in Merrill Court and there was no taboo against talk about it. Six residents died in the course of my three years of field work, and many non-resident friends and older relatives also died in that time. Although each individual faced death essentially alone, there was a collective concern with, as they put it, "being ready" and facing up, a concern the young could not share with them in quite the same way. The deaths of fellow residents meant a great deal to the community and they reveal a great deal about it. Strangely enough, five of the six deaths happened to people who had their social and psychic "boots on." For example, Rosie, an active club officer, died half an hour after returning from a Bible study class. Another two died while arranging with

---

* The widows felt they were needed by the other widows. One declared, "One thing about bein' here, you're missed when you go on a trip. I write letters and get letters sayin' 'come back soon.' " On her return from summer visits, she was annually greeted at the railroad station by the Merrill Court band.

someone on the telephone for a meeting the following week. One died peacefully in bed and another in a chair, both after a day of activities. Only the sixth died in a hospital after a few days of not feeling well and inactivity.

Among the widows, there was a "good" and a "bad" way to die. Rosie's death especially was the community's example of "the right way to die." She was praised as much for remaining active to the end as for "being ready" in both the practical and philosophic sense. Her will and burial were prearranged and she was on good terms with "her people." As they looked around them, some residents were said to be "living on borrowed time" while others had not "lived out their mission." But whatever the case, they were agreed that one should try to face death rather than turn one's back on it,[4] all while living fully to the end.

One way to become "ready" in a community such as this is to observe the death of another person. I would like to focus on the death of Rosie and on what it meant for the other widows, individually and as a community.

Rosie had been an active member of the community and her sudden death took everyone by surprise. In reconstructing the events leading to her death, the widows studied the details of all their last encounters with her. Someone volunteered:

> I saw her in the elevator coming up from Bible meeting. She talked about the bazaar we were having Friday. We waved good-bye. That was the last I saw her.

They discussed why she had said "goodbye" instead of "good-night" and reviewed her habitual way of signing off with friends to try to discover whether she had known that she would die.

Immediately the community held an emergency meeting to arrange for the funeral supper. The flower committee* ordered

---

* There was some disagreement about whether to spend all the flower money for the funeral or to save some for her birthday and Memorial Day. But in the face of death, issues that threatened to divide the community were quickly passed over.

a $15 wreath and many volunteered to cook a dish for the be-
reaved relatives. A cold supper was arranged for thirty-five relatives and friends. Nearly everyone in the community went to
view the body at a local funeral parlor, to the funeral service, and
to the burial.* In the following week there was a moratorium on
work, as became the custom with deaths in the building. These
customs gave those left a chance to cry, to express sorrow,[5] to
comfort, and to be comforted without fear of embarrassment; and
it gave them a chance to *do* something—call people, buy flowers,
bake pies.

In this way the community taught itself about death. Although they were part of a collectivity that was itself immortal
and in which the deceased were replaced, they each realized their
own mortality. In going to the funerals of others, it is as if they
were experimentally going to their own.

In many ways, the community protected the dead in ways in
which the young do not. For example, when Mr. Cooper, the
only senile person in the community, died, it was noted:

> The funeral was in ————. He didn't have any friends, poor
> dear. But five or six from here went and we got him some
> flowers. Oh, they were lovely flowers.

The community also turned out for the funeral of another person
whose only daughter lived abroad and could not be there. Although he did not live in the building and was only a bare ac-
quaintance to most of the residents, twenty of them went "to sign
the book" in order, as they put it, "to show his wife we cared." **

---

* It was in a preselected plot on a large rolling hill overlooking the
freeway below and tract homes on all sides. Some plastic flowers were
arranged on the grave. The group lingered a while at the grave, after
others had left. Another Catholic resident requested a mass to be
said for her, though when the mass was said three months later (due to
a backlog), few of the Protestant residents went. This was a source
of much discussion.
** In other respects the dead are mentally dismissed. In my intial inter-
views with the residents, I asked how many brothers and sisters they

The widows also kept an eye on how others—friends, acquaintances, and professionals—reacted to death. They noticed how much friendship that seemed to matter during life was expressed after death. The death of one neighboring non-resident was much deplored. The woman, who had been in fine health, had gone to the hospital and unexpectedly died there. As one Merrill Court widow reported it:

> She had lovely, expensive roses planted in her backyard. She had promised them to her neighbor for when she died. Well, she was taken to the hospital, and the day her death was announced, before she was buried, that neighbor was digging up those roses, saying Mrs. ———— had promised them to her.

The widow related the case from the point of view of the deceased, not from the point of view of the callous neighbor, or widowed husband. But what distressed the group even more than the alienated behavior of the neighbor was the fact that the deceased had not known that she was about to die.

The widows also watched how funeral parlor personnel and insurance companies reacted to the death of loved ones. One mentioned indignantly that her insurance company had refused to cover her husband because his health report was poor. Another brought out that the funeral parlor people had charged them for a more elaborate funeral than they asked for or could afford. She remarked, "There's an English lady who wrote something about funerals." * Another commented that when her hus-

---

had. In response, many mentioned only *living* siblings. That is, "I have three brothers" actually meant "I have three brothers alive." It was only from later conversations that I reconstructed the kinship structure as it was in their youth. We might infer from this the way in which the widows expect to be regarded when their time comes. They talk frequently about the kind of funeral they want ("I want roses," or "I don't want flowers, I want a plaque."), but I seldom heard them talk about how they would be missed years later.

* She was referring to Jessica Mitford's *The American Way of Death* (1963). Most of the residents knew about the book, although none had read it.

band died, the landlady had been angry, because she did not think she could rent the apartment out since there had been a death in it. In such little chilling ways, the widows learn how others think of death.

The community tried to reduce the unpredictability of death by guessing how long a person had to live* and by trying to tell if the deceased had foretold her death. One woman said of Rosie, "I think she knew. She had all her Christmas gifts bought and wrapped by the 11th of December." But another added, "Well, I had all my gifts wrapped too. I had Merry Christmas written on twenty socks, and I didn't have any premonition like that!" Myths also reduced the upsetting unpredictability of death. As one resident described:

> It's a strange thing, but when Mr. Cooper died, Dorie took up the flower collection. And then she was the next to go. And when she died, Rosie took up the collection, and then she died. Now that we see what's happening, no one wants to take up the collection.

Although there was joking on this point, the last volunteer agreed to collect for flowers only if the Recreation Director did it with her. Strange to say, empirically the pattern was not a myth. There was in these cases a link between collecting for the flower fund and being the next to die. What *made* it a myth was the causal connection between collecting the money and dying.

---

* Glaser and Strauss (1965) refer to this as "establishing trajectories." Such trajectories were often inaccurate. For example, Emma, an 80-year-old homesteader from Oklahoma, had gone back and forth between Merrill Court and a nursing home three times, each predicted to be her last. As a neigbor commented, "She came home from the nursing home yesterday, sharp as a tack. I'll be honest, I didn't expect to see her again." Because Emma was formerly so active, her sudden turn for the worse was interpreted as a signal of approaching death, although, as it turned out, it was not. On the other hand, Daisy had never been active and her monthly trips between Merrill Court and the hospital caused no alarm; "Oh, Daisy's feeling fairly well, the way she has for the last half year. Her time isn't up yet."

There was perhaps a link between a premonition of personal death and caring about someone else's. It is important here because of what the pattern meant to the community, and because the topic never seemed to arise in age-integrated company.

Another topic the widows discussed among themselves was "apparitions," something young people normally do not experience.[6] On one occasion, when the women were working and talking downstairs, someone mentioned that when she was alone up in her apartment she sometimes had the impression of a "presence" of someone dead in the room. "It's so real you almost want to speak." The others nodded in agreement and commented, "It makes you wonder." To two of them, the presence took the form of an apparition. To five others it was just a presence, as if everything but the body of the person were in the room. When questioned individually later, they said that sometimes it made them happy, but most of the time it made them sad to realize that the absent person could never really be there. Some of them felt the presence of Rosie, mentioned earlier, others that of their recently deceased relative, but oddly enough, rarely that of their husbands.* Almost all of them dream about friends or relatives who have passed away. These ways of reinvoking the dead were spoken of with hushed voices, and a joke usually turned the conversation in another direction.

Although the widows talked about the events leading up to death and death itself frankly, in detail, and even in a matter-of-fact way, they seldom mentioned what happened to the body afterward. It is as if the taboo that for young people stops before death, is for old people moved beyond it. On one occasion the topic arose from the discussion of an atheist who had appeared on a television program. The discussion of atheism led to a discus-

---

* This may reflect a greater distance between spouses in this class than others. Many studies of working-class marriages mention the separate spheres of husband and wife. It may be this situation that enables the widows of Merrill Court to form a community so readily. This might be harder for the widowed in the upper-middle class, where the husband and wife are closer.

sion of God and religion, which in turn led to a discussion of science and donating bodies to science. One woman commented:

> Now they's a few who want to have their bodies cremated. I can't see no sense in that. Who'd want that? Now I told the doctor if my body could be of use to science, I'd let them use it. If I could be of help in preventing others from suffering what I've got, I'd do it.

But as soon as this subject was mentioned someone wanted to know, "How did we get on this subject? This is *depressing.*" And the discussion promptly ended. Although death was not considered "depressing," the use of one's physical remains was.* Beyond a common-sense interpretation, it is worth looking at the difference in their minds between the two things. Death was spoken of as being like sleep. Talk about disposal of one's bodily remains makes it seem much less like sleep. Furthermore, there is nothing a bereaved person can *do* about that aspect of death to relieve his own feelings of loss.

Death is significant to the old in a way it is not to the young, not only because old people are nearer to their own death but because they are nearer to other people's. Both young and old suffer loss through death but the old are more exposed to death than the young and exposed through different social channels. In pre-modern societies, death was as much associated with youth as it was with old age.[7] It is only in modern societies, with advanced medicine and reduced mortality rates for the young, that most people could expect to live through their youth and middle age and die only in old age. It is only under these modern conditions that the old become society's "shock absorber" of death.

---

* On one trip that the club took to the Ice Follies in San Francisco, there was singing on the bus both coming and going. They sang some old-time songs, including "On Top of Old Smokey." One line in the song goes, "And the grave will decay you and turn you to dust, not one man in a hundred a poor girl can trust." When the singers reached this line they all came to a halt and there were some objecting remarks until a new song was started—"When You and I Were Young, Maggie."

Outside the family, the old person's friends are mainly other old people and a young person's friends are mainly other young people. Because in America one age group is divided from another, confining friendships within age boundaries, it is the old whose friends die. If friendships outside the family were evenly distributed throughout the age scale, young people would face loss through death as much as old people do. As it is, the old have become a "buffer zone" between society and death. On the other hand, *within the family*, this age-separation is broken by the parent-child chain linking each generation to the next. Thus, death confronts the old mainly through their bonds to old friends outside the family. It affects the young mainly through their family ties to grandparents and parents and older relatives.

In Merrill Court, very rarely did the topic of death come up in the presence of kin or young people, and I would like to suggest a possible reason for this. Geoffrey Gorer, in his essay "The Pornography of Death," points out that death is replacing sex as the new "unmentionable." Compared to our nineteenth-century predecessors, we are more prudish about death, whereas sex, another natural process, is more open to frank discussion. Death and decay are considered as "disgusting" as birth and copulation were a century ago—a new "not before the children" sort of thing.

Death and sexual love are two crucial experiences, death having to do with the end of life, sexual love with the beginning; death having to do with separation, sexual love with union. Both evoke powerful, potentially disruptive and unmanageable feelings. Parallel to the sexual urge are the emotions of grief, guilt, and a sense of abandonment that one feels at the death of a loved one. A taboo handles these threatening feelings by avoiding them. In the nineteenth century, people saw more of death and had rituals to handle the feelings it aroused. In the twentieth century, except in communities such as this one, it seems there is an uneasiness and avoidance of talk about death.

However, just as the former taboo on sex tended to be lifted in age-segregated company, so too perhaps the taboo on death is lifted in age-segregated company. Men alone together and women alone together, even in the Victorian age, may have talked about sex more freely. In a similar way, the old among the old feel freer to talk about death. There are probably many old people who do not talk about death as freely as do the widows of Merrill Court. But the sibling solidarity there tends to liberate the topic of death, to allow straightforward, non-euphemistic language, to open the unembarrassed expression of grief, and to support the task of mourning. Only a small proportion of old people live in such old age communities, but it is probably true that in general the old among the old feel less constrained to deny aging and death or to observe the taboo on talk related to them.

Between the young and the old and between parent and child, on the other hand, the taboo seems to be stronger. Comments such as "You look ten years younger" or "You don't look a day over 50" make it difficult to face this stage of life squarely. Unlike the old, the young are not yet themselves faced with the reality of personal death, and it is not relevant to them in the same way. They are not brothers in the same boat; they are abandoned children. For the young, and even more for the middle aged, the older parent in relinquishing his parenthood forces the younger to relinquish his childhood.[8] It does not in the same way alter the relation of the old who have already reconciled themselves to the disappearance of childhood. It seems to be the young who, for their own reasons, enforce the taboo.

chapter five

FAMILY TIES AND MOTHERLY LOVE

"The family feeling which led him to cherish the past history of his house extended itself even more strongly into his future; and he was influenced, too, by the loving and expectant curiosity concentrated upon his son by his family and his friends and acquaintances . . . He said to himself that, however hopeless and thwarted he himself felt, he was still, wherever his son was concerned, capable of inexhaustible streams of energy, endurance, achievement, success . . ."

> *Buddenbrooks*
> by Thomas Mann, translated by H. T. Lowe-Porter.
> orig. 1901, 1952, pp. 483–84.
>
> Reprinted by permission of Alfred A. Knopf, Inc.

A quick thought might tell us that the stronger the bonds the old have with one another, the weaker their ties to family. Indeed, American sociologist Arnold Rose[1] has suggested that the more kin ties there are, the fewer peer ties there will be. But even a flat-footed contrast of contacts with relatives and with peers suggests that this is not true at Merrill Court. Beyond that, the two relationships differ in a qualitative way; the sibling bond with neighbors seems to emerge only when relations with children are "in order." As we have seen, when institutional living transforms the old into "patient-children," the sibling bond with fellow patients fails to emerge. On the other hand, if the parent-child bond does not exist at all, research suggests that then, too, siblings cannot replace it. In the following, I shall try to show why this might be.

The grandmothers see a lot of their relatives; about nine out of ten see some child at least once a week and two-thirds see or talk to one every day. In this respect the grandmothers are surprisingly like grandparents everywhere in the United States.[2] Children are perhaps especially important because other kinds of relatives have, with history, become less so. In a traditional society, the grandparent is at the apex of a genealogical tree where genealogy itself is the social cement. But very few at Merrill Court were "connecting relatives," [3] since those who would be connected by a grandparent or great-grandparent—first and second cousins, uncles, and aunts—are no longer themselves part of a cohesive unit.*

Since most had several children spread across the country, there was a yearly mass exodus from Merrill Court to points East, which created a lull in club affairs from June to September. All year each widow saved money for bus or plane fare and before the trip she shopped for a new dress or coat, comparing buys. Some went on anticipatory diets and most spent a long, slow time packing. One woman was fondly teased for taking three months to pack for a fishing trip with her son's family. A few days before departure, they went to the hairdresser for a "perm" and maybe a "dye," something they seldom did when offstage among themselves. Those who did not go visiting would admire the perm, help with the packing, and finally wait for the postcards.

But most of their children lived nearby; about six out of ten had at least one child living right in town and most of the rest

---

* One exception in Merrill Court was Emma Fieldstone, a farmer's wife, who would, at the slightest suggestion, show off the photographs of her 80th birthday party to which some eighty kin were gathered from all over the country to honor her. This was much admired among the peers, but unmatched. Most of the grandmothers did not, even symbolically, connect members of the whole clan with one another, but they did connect their immediate children with one another.

had children in the outlying suburbs.* They talked of being "hollerin' distance away," but of course they didn't holler, they called. (Many talked in loud voices, even in the Recreation Room. This was not connected with hearing difficulties, and it may be a "culture lag" from the days of shouting across a barnyard, carried over into an urban setting.)

Women have traditionally bound the generations together, and in Merrill Court it is the daughters who most often visit and call. There was a saying there: "If you have a daughter, you have her for life. If you have a son, you lose him to a wife." [4] A visit to a daughter typically involved sitting out on the lawn at the daughter's home, over a cup of coffee, inspecting the new home appliances, or interior decorating, or boat-building projects. It might also mean a shopping visit or giving or getting a home permanent wave. If the "daughter for life" happened to work, as many did, the grandmothers often saw more of a daughter-in-law who did not. In two cases, a daughter who worked outside the home gave the grandmother work outside her home. These two grandchildren were often taken on outings and bowling with the grandmothers, and they were collective property inside the Recreation Room.

Most grandmothers approved of their daughters' working: "You can't manage these days on just the one salary." But one woman who had worked on the farm most of her life commented:

> These women today go out and work. They could get along without it, so their kids would be reared up right. They could grow cabbages and carrots in their backyards and make do. . . . I've worked all my life but I had an eye on ma young.

The grandmothers liked to visit their children, but as they often put it, they "wouldn't want to live there." All but four

---

* Typically, a third to a half of their children lived nearby. The grandmother with the most children (eleven) had eight in the area and three back in Texas and Oklahoma. The grandmother with the fewest (one) lived "hollerin'" distance away. The average for the building was 3.9 children and 22 percent had over six.

strongly opposed the idea of living with their children, including ten who had tried it within the last ten years. One woman who moved in with her daughter's family after her husband died had this to say:

> Most of the people here feel like I do. I don't want to be living with my kids. I love them. I don't want to have, you know, any misunderstandings. Why, if I were to live there, I couldn't have friends in so easy or cook on my stove. They have their friends and the kids have their friends. It's better all 'round, just visiting and being close.*

Physical separation did not mean emotional distance. On the contrary, most had not only close but what they called "good," emotionally rewarding relations with their children. I know of only five exceptions, two of whom had close but "bad" relations. The adoptive daughter of one grandmother had turned to drink and become more and more isolated. The other regularly called her daughter and son but resented them bitterly. But the bitterness had two sides and a history. After her husband died, Ada left her farm in Wisconsin—and eight small children—to come to California and work as a tank cleaner in the shipyards. She was the only resident who fit Edward Albee's description, in *The American Dream*, of the plight of the old. As she put it,

> I have three children nearby and they don't have time for Grandma. Grandma don't count. My daughter-in-law, she calls me every night, they call all right but they don't visit and they don't ask me to visit them. They go fishing on the weekends and either it's too hot for me to come or it's too cold for me to come or the fish ain't bitin'. Well, I can sit and wait for those fish to bite as well as they can. I don't like it. I sit by the phone on Satur-

* She added, "It wouldn't have worked in my day, either. Each generation has to live its own way. We moved when we had to, when Bill got the job at the railroad, when he had his heart attack, and when we came out here to be near Angela (a daughter). You have to think of your own family." This is interesting in light of the fact that a quarter of the residents whose parents lived to be old, lived with and cared for their parents in old age.

day and they say, "We tried to call you." I've had enough of that stuff. Grandma don't count. I'm gonna take a trip to Wisconsin and I'm not going to tell them. Let them worry for once.

Although most of the widows sympathized with Ada, she was not in their eyes quite a "poor dear," for, as they remarked offhandedly in her absence, "You reap what you sow."

Ada was a staunch supporter of an "exclusion policy" toward the kin when potlucks and "dime a dip" suppers* were given downstairs. This attitude suggests that those with unhappy (though not necessarily weak) family ties may seek something different—such as revenge—in their peer relations.**

But is it true that those with weak family ties made up for it with peer ties? The question is not so simple as it sounds, as a look at the interactional surface of the two bonds shows. Bonds with kin were most of the time managed separately from bonds with peers. By keeping the two contexts separate, loyalties were kept separate too. In this way the grandmothers resembled the widows in Charlotte Armstrong's novel *The Seventeen Widows of Sans Souci*:

> The division was understood. Whenever one of them had visitors—relatives or old friends from back home—the other widows of Sans Souci by a never mentioned convention would keep away. Not many of those being visited attempted to bring the two lives together. It was not that the relatives . . . could not have met the new "friends" in the building and been mutu-

---

* A buffet supper with many dishes prepared by different residents. The number of ten-cent helpings on one's plate determined the cost, usually very low.
** Perhaps the peer group performs a latent function of "letting off steam" that cannot be expressed in the family. Because the old have no authority in the family, hostile feelings may not be so openly expressed there. But these feelings were expressed among peers, and it was considered something a problem. Thus perhaps some of the hostility generated in the family was displaced from family to peers, much as sibling rivalry can have an element of hostility whose original target was a parent.

ally polite. It was as if the widows were each two women and the mixing of the two selves was what might be confusing.[5]

In Merrill Court, too, relatives brought out "another self." Nevertheless the two selves, the two lives, were in some ways integrated. For example, when a daughter came to Merrill Court to take her mother shopping, to the hairdresser, or to drop off groceries, she was often told the latest activities in the community. Again, after one woman was elected President of the Service Club, she remarked, "I can't wait to tell my kids about this." Thus, the status earned in the peer community carried over into family life. Among themselves the old often discussed their kin, and, as suggested earlier, the more children, the higher their status in the old age community. Residents showed off and shared their visiting relatives.

Only the obese daughter of Beatrice, the piano player, regularly attended the Monday morning Service Club meetings and was her mother's only ally there. Other kin came in mainly on special occasions—at the installation of officers, birthday parties, potlucks, and Christmas. Sometimes the grandmothers rounded up their grandchildren to serve at the table, but only on important occasions when they thought it unseemly for club members to be getting up and around during the meal. On most club trips to shows and movies there was a sprinkling of grandchildren.

Kin also provided services to the grandmothers. One daughter worked in a beauty parlor and, disobeying union rules, gave home permanents for a moderate price to her mother's friends at Merrill Court. Another son-in-law worked in an upholstery company and supplied scraps of cloth to be worked into rag dolls for the bazaar. Another son was a plumber and occasionally fixed dripping faucets. Two granddaughters cleaned their grandmothers' apartments every week, and were paid for it.

In one case, a granddaughter, a typist nearby, stayed overnight with her grandmother on weekends. The granddaughter was not shared with the other residents but she shared *her* outside life with her grandmother, Delia. I will report on this situation because it updates Richard Hoggart's study of the English working class, *The Uses of Literacy*. In that book, Hoggart noted that parents and grandparents often evaluate a prospective son-in-law while conversing with him in the family living room. Delia carried this function with her to Merrill Court. Her three granddaughters frequently brought their boy friends to watch television in Delia's apartment. This gave Delia a chance to "pass inspection" and report back to the parents. The evaluations were based not so much on direct talk as on the boy's reactions to television programs. The granddaughter and her boy friend would usually sit in back of the grandmother, presumably for romantic purposes, everyone facing the TV. Delia summed up her evaluation of the boy this way:

> Ricky's not a good person for Kathy. We were watching a cowboy show yesterday evening. There was one point in the story where a little boy was asked by the ranchers where the hero was. Ricky didn't like the hero. He wanted those ranchers to get the information out of that little boy. He wanted the outlaws to win.*

Thus, not only were kin drawn into Merrill Court, kin pulled the residents outside it. "Visiting" or "seeing mine" was a legitimate excuse for getting out of doing something. When one commitment conflicted with another, kin ties usually won over peer ties—but not always without a struggle. On one occasion Delia and Rosie were playing their weekly game of marbles with a married couple on the same floor. As Delia recounted:

> Iffy's daughter is very demanding. We were there, as guests. We were playing marbles and Barbara [Iffy's daughter] called on

---

* She was also dismayed that Ricky enjoyed the violence. In general, the grandmothers knew quite a lot about their grandchildren but their knowledge was selective. They knew more about their current romances than about their classes or jobs—at least as far as their granddaughters were concerned. Delia was especially close to her granddaughter and had what she called "an open closet": "Sometimes I get ready to wear my yellow sweater and it's gone from the closet. I tell my granddaughters they can borrow whatever they need. And they do."

the phone to invite them [the couple] over for some watermelon. Iffy told her, she said, "We have guests just now. We'll be along over later." But Barbara called up ten minutes later and asked when they were coming. Barbara knows how long a game takes. We didn't think that was nice, insisting like that when we were visiting.

In eleven other similar instances reported in my field notes, kin ties won and peer ties lost. A child's leisure is hemmed in by work but a marbles game with age peers can always be arranged for another night.

In a few cases kin ties won out altogether. For example, Laura, who played the washtub bass in the band but complained bitterly about the $3 yearly dues, planned to move out of Merrill Court to live in a trailer on her son's farm:

I don't like it here much. I can't do my canning and fishing and you can't raise chickens here . . . can't even have a dog. I lived in the trailer once before I came here. Reckon I can do it again. I visit them [her children] a lot. They want me to stay.

Although relations with kin and with peers were sometimes brought together, on the whole they were kept separate. When they were brought together they usually did not conflict. But when they did conflict, kin ties usually won. This pattern held true for women with both strong ties to family *and* to peers—and that included almost everyone. The few whose family ties were feebly held together by Christmas cards and graduation notices did not "make up for it" by plunging themselves into Merrill Court affairs. They, like Vera, the religious woman, remained aloof from the subculture as well. Moreover, those who had especially strong and rewarding family ties were—like Delia, whose granddaughters courted in her living room—always on the phone or downstairs arranging for the bazaar or the Bowling Club banquet. In fact, with the ambiguous exception of Laura, those closest to their families were among the most active in Merrill Court society.[6]

In a deep sense and over the long run, the two kinds of relationships did not really compete; one could not replace the other even in the "time filling" sense. To the widows, children are a socio-emotional insurance policy that peers can never be. Kin ties run deeper and have a longer history than peer ties. When a grandmother is in deep trouble, she turns to blood ties first. When a widow needs a lot of money, she turns to kin; when she needs "something to tide her over till payday," she turns to a neighbor. When there was an accident or death in the building, peers were the first to find out, but kin were the first to be called.

Whereas relationships between peers had a "tit for tat" exchange of goods and services, relations with kin were not, in the strictly economic sense, reciprocal.[7] Children usually gave their parents—through money for a doctor's bill, part of the rent, a new sofa or rug—slightly more than they got back. The grandmothers, in partial return, knitted Christmas socks, baked cakes, or bought a prom dress or class ring for a grandchild.

This latent economic dimension in parent-child relations distinguishes it from peer relations. Most of the transfer of money from one generation to another goes on *outside* the family context, since the taxes middle-aged people pay go to meet the money claims of the old and the young.[8] A number of grandmothers saw the matter in precisely these terms. Ernestine, for example, who received social security benefits and old age assistance, remarked,

> I didn't want to put in for old age but then my son said, "I don't begrudge any money to you, but if you can get a little help, don't feel bad about it." So I put in for "Old Age."

Ernestine linked the "prosperity" of some residents to the taxes her son was paying:

> There are two people in this building who never worked. They just raised their families, you know. And their husbands were never on social security—they were farmers, see, and they didn't have social security in the country back then. And these two women, I'm not mentioning any names, get nine dollars more a month than Freda and me who lived in the city and paid social

security. And on "Old Age" they ask for rugs and bedroom sets and Old Age pays most of that. You have to pay the difference if it's over a certain amount. My son pays $800 in taxes each year. Of course most of that goes to the schools. But some of it goes to Old Age.

According to Ernestine, her son was supporting the two drones in the building who lived on Old Age payments and got more money than she. She discussed the problem with Freda and with her social worker, but found no justification for the injustice. She found herself in the odd position of identifying with her son as a taxpayer and receiving the benefit of taxes herself. She reasoned that it was, in part, her own son who was paying the benefits she received each month, but by the same token, she resented the portion he paid that went to other old people.

Parallel to the economic dependence that distinguished the grandmothers' relations with children from those with peers was an emotional dependence of a very special identity-branding kind. The widow's identity at this point in her life seemed to be like this: "I am my children's mother, my grandchildren's grandmother, my peers' friend, my late husband's wife, my doctor's patient, the club's officer, my welfare worker's client, my deceased friend's friend, and my ex co-worker's buddy." Both within Merrill Court and outside it, "my daughter's mother" was a most important source of identity.

The relationship of grandmother to daughter often goes by the name of love. But it explains little to call it that. In what was called love, I found time and again evidence of projection and identification.[9] By identification, I mean perceiving another person as an extension of oneself. What follows is based on an intensive study of the ten grandmothers on the third floor and their relations with one of their children. Of the ten, nine seemed to identify strongly with a relative: six with a daughter, two with a granddaughter, and one with a grandson. I shall not talk about these relationships in general, but only about the quality of them that suggests identification and projection.

One thing that literary critics dwell on in novels is the *point of view* from which a story is told. That is useful for sociologists to consider too. I mentioned earlier how Delia described the death of a neighbor from the deceased neighbor's point of view. Ernestine, in the example above, spoke of her son's tax payments from *his* point of view, even while she and everyone around her was a tax recipient, not payer. Again, when the widows told stories of their past, it was often from the perspective of how they must have seemed to *older* people then. For example, Irma described herself as a 14-year-old girl: "I was a wild thing in those days. I must have been a headache for my father. I don't know how he managed." The speaker talked *as if* she had adopted the eyes and mind of another. We can sometimes infer identification from a direct, "If I were he (or she) I would . . ." statement, but more often it is indirect. For example, the widows often responded to shampoo or face cream advertisements on television by mentioning how a daughter might react to the same item. Typically they would not say, "That's a nice shampoo, Lucy should use it," but rather, "Now Lucy would probably go out and buy that." What is critical here is not the fact that the widows talked about their daughters, which they did at length, but *how* they talked about them. What I often heard was not a description of the daughter's life from the grandmother's point of view, but a description of the daughter's life from the grandmother's version of the daughter's point of view.

The case of one grandmother illustrates the kind of love the other grandmothers had for their children and grandchildren. Delia had three children—one daughter living nearby who was married to a railroad man and had three daughters, one 40-year-old divorced daughter who worked for the Social Security Administration in San Francisco, and a son who was a teacher in Illinois. Of the three, Delia talked most, and most animatedly, about her first daughter.*

This daughter, Angela, had three daughters. The family recently had moved from a home in Verada, only five minutes drive from Merrill Court, to a new home in the expanding sub-

---

* Perhaps the norm that parents should love all their offspring equally is to some extent broken in old age.

urb of Camalita about fifty miles away. The new home had modern conveniences such as a built-in washer and dryer, a larger backyard, and a two-car garage. It was also in a *de facto* racially segregated neighborhood, although this was never mentioned (to me).

Angela and her family talked about the move with great anticipation; in her life it was, as she put it, "a dream come true." But it also meant that the two girls living at home would have to live apart from their parents in order to be near their jobs in Verada. It meant, too, that Delia, the grandmother, would probably visit and call her daughter less often, though for slightly longer—because of the expense of a long-distance call and the hour's drive. Delia had no car and the family had only one. Delia normally received a daily telephone call from her daughter and usually two or three semi-surprise visits during the week. Under the new arrangement Delia came and stayed for a weekend once a month or so. While the three generations were thus geographically separated, Angela and her husband made the move with a neighboring couple their own age from Verada.

Delia reacted to this news in the following way: After each call from Angela reporting on the latest details of the move, Delia would telephone a friend in the building and discuss the latest report. She knew the size of the new lot, the dimensions of the living room and bedrooms, the arrangement of facilities in the kitchen. She would discuss with Angela and other friends at Merrill Court the relative merits of a beige versus an emerald green rug for the living room, the kind of curtain material to use in the bedrooms, and landscaping ideas for the yard. In describing the new house to the neighbor she remarked:

> I just know how Angela feels. She must be thrilled. There will be an eye-level oven in the kitchen, an avocado green. I can just picture it. That'll be nice for her baking on Thursdays. It's just what they've wanted. I'm so happy *for* her.

What is striking about this example is that if anything, Delia herself stood to lose from the new arrangement, but by identifying with her daughter in the new house, she was pleased by it. It was almost as if Delia *herself* were moving in rather than simply sharing the lifestyle mobility. In conversation she often talked interchangeably about her daughter's move to the new house and her own move to a new house in Iowa when she was first married. "I remember I was so pleased that we had running water and didn't have to pump it up like we did on the farm. Oh, I loved the stove we had in that house." She also compared the relationship she and her husband had had with a neighboring couple with the relationship of her daughter and husband with their neighbors.

Delia described her daughter's oven in such a way as to give the listener the impression that the young body and the old were interchangeable, that a sort of transmigration of the soul had occurred. This identification comes close to Anna Freud's description of "altruistic surrender." In her book *The Ego and the Mechanisms of Defense,* she described the case history of a young governess who as a child wanted to have beautiful clothes and a number of children, but as an adult had neither—though she *identified* with those who did. It is worth describing the case in some detail:

> The repudiation of her own sexuality did not prevent her from taking an affectionate interest in the love life of her women friends and colleagues. She was an enthusiastic matchmaker and many love affairs were confided to her. Although she took no trouble about her own dress, she displayed a lively interest in her friends' clothes. Childless herself, she was devoted to other people's children, as was indicated by her choice of profession. She might be said to display an unusual degree of concern about her friends having pretty clothes, being admired, and having children. Similarly, in spite of her own retiring behavior, she was ambitious for the men whom she loved and followed their careers with the utmost interest. It looked as if her own life had been emptied of interest and wishes; up to the time of her analysis it was almost entirely uneventful. Instead of exerting herself to achieve any aim of her own, she expended all her energy in sympathizing with the experiences of people she cared for. She lived in the

lives of other people, instead of having any experience of her own.[10]

According to Anna Freud, impulses that appeared impossible to fulfill were not in this case repressed. Rather, the patient found a proxy in the outside world to serve as a repository for them. She gratified her instincts by ". . . sharing in the gratification of others, employing for this purpose the mechanisms of projection and identification." [11]

Altruistic surrender is probably more evident among the old whose own life, like that of the governess, is relatively uneventful. That we find this condition among the grandmothers of Merrill Court, whose "other" life is anything but uneventful, suggests the remarkable power of the mechanism. We should expect to find it *even more* in older people who have no on-going interests of their own.[12]

To perceive another as an extension of oneself is to risk some ambiguity in the psychic boundary between the identifier and the identified-with. All nine grandmothers at times talked of their children as the sum result of their own parental effort, not as a result of the child's own evolving capacities, even when the "child" was middle aged. (One grandmother often referred to "my baby," who turned out to be a 50-year-old garage owner.)

The successes of their children they often ascribed to them-selves, *even* when these successes could not in a simple way be ascribed to the children themselves. For example, the grand-mothers lived on small farms, in small towns or in the dingy city districts, whereas their children live in modest but larger homes with neatly manicured lawns and own monumental cars. Whereas the grandmothers had an average of six years of edu-cation, their daughters have an average of ten. However, with an average annual income of $8,000, the children probably did just as well, but no better, than *their* cohorts in the population. Since there has been a structural trend from rural to urban occu-pations, from unskilled to skilled, and since the mobility rate is particularly high in California, the children's mobility is "structural" rather than "individual." [13] Nevertheless, not only do the children take exclusively personal credit for their mobility, their grandmothers do too, claiming it to be a result and payoff for their own labors.* As one grandmother put it, "I raised my kids up. I put them all through school. It was a lot of hard work, but they come out good." Another remarked about her son, a plumber, "He makes good money now. I guess all those years paid off." Thus, not only do the sons and daughters themselves translate structural mobility into private terms, the grandmothers vicariously do too. Perhaps in an age of structural downward mobility a similar group of grandmothers would assume indirect personal blame for structural failure.

To identify with a child and to acknowledge the integrity of his or her adulthood are related but separate phenomena. A mother can take some credit or blame—i.e., responsibilty—for a success without identifying with the child, and can identify without taking reponsibility. Furthermore, a grandmother's taking credit could vary with the context; she might fantasize, "All she has achieved is mine," but deal with her daughter's concrete presence in quite another way.

I would now like to elaborate on the meaning of altruistic surrender for what it says about the grandmothers and about *other* socially deprived groups. Altruistic surrender requires a person willing to be altruistically surrendered *to*. In all these cases, the identified-with agreed to it or did not object. The daughters provided the intimate details of their lives and filled

---

* The grandmothers took personal credit in a broader sense for the very technological innovations that have made their past labor unnecessary. One woman (Daisy) who had recently watched a television program featuring Rap Brown, the black leader, concluded, "We elders built up this push button stuff. That fellow Rap Brown said that he made the good life and now he's burning it down. That's not right. The elder people built it up and now the young people are tearing it down. It's not right." Daisy was in a minority in her opinion that the young people actually were tearing down "the push button stuff," but with three exceptions, all the residents took full credit for the general technological progress of the age despite the fact that their occupations had had little to do with technological innovation.

their mothers in on every change of plan and new event, not retrospectively but as they were happening. Thus, like a movie in which the viewer is let in on all the episodes and feelings that propel the protagonist to his destiny, so the grandmothers knew their identified-with child.

This may account for the fact that the grandmothers of Merrill Court were singularly uninterested in young people *in general*. The Recreation Leader repeatedly suggested working in a day care center or an orphanage as a club project, and each time the idea met an unfriendly or indifferent reception. They were more interested in serving other old people than young people. This suggests that not all young people are liked simply for their youth, but only the young with whom identification can be established. Altruistic surrender is probably not always confined to blood relatives but it picks its object carefully.

There is one more characteristic of altruistic surrender that is perhaps more important, although least visible. In her analysis of the governess, Anna Freud pointed out that the patient at one point converted intense envy into identification.* This response suggests an interesting link between identification and envy. According to the *Random House Dictionary*, envy means "a feeling of discontent or jealousy, usually with ill will, at seeing another's superiority, advantage or success," and "desire for some advantage possessed by another." For our purposes, the stress on ill will is important. Altruistic surrender involves desiring some advantage possessed by another, *without* experiencing ill will toward the advantaged person. Quite the contrary, it involves more than good will toward that person.

Possibly when envy is, for whatever reason, not tolerable, identification is its more acceptable substitute. More precisely, envy with "ill will" may be substituted for envy with "good will."

---

* "She had projected her own desire for love and her craving for admiration onto her rival and, having identified herself with the object of her envy, she enjoyed the fulfillment of her desire." (A. Freud, 1966, p. 127.) However, one does not necessarily envy all those with whom one identifies nor does one identify with all those whom one envies.

There is little discussion in scholarly works on envy between older generations, although of course Freud has pointed out that in the Oedipal conflict, the father envies the young son and the mother her daughter as well as vice versa. I saw no evidence from which I could infer envy in the relations between these grandmothers and their daughters. That is, I saw no overt envy. However, it is certainly not impossible that Delia herself would have liked a new eye-level avocado colored oven and twenty more years of life in which to enjoy it.

To maintain social cohesion it is probably important to contain envy between generations and between males and females— two strata of human beings that have to get along together if society is to survive.* We seldom think of envy as a "problem" precisely because these strata usually do get along; divisions are more typically within these strata than between them, divorce and the generation gap notwithstanding. For example, the family is held together by love between husband and wife and parents and children. However, if we inspect various loves we find that they differ in the element of identification.** This identification is often "one-way." That is, the woman often lives through the man, partaking of his public life and success in a way that the man does not live through the woman in return. The old often live through the young, partaking of their adventure and success, in a way that the young do not live through the old in return. Thus the husband's success becomes the wife's success and the

---

* Rivalry and envy are often handled through identification. Identification can be one functional alternative to competition for scarce rewards. There may be some link between the accommodating political styles of "the good Negro," the "wife who knows her place," and the "graceful ager," all of whom are for one reason or another cooled out of the competitive arena of a young, white male world, and all of whom *identify* with those in the arena—blacks with whites, women with men, and old with young. (See K. Davis, 1940, 1966.)

** I mean identification not in the sense of being identified *by* another, but identifying *with* another. Dependents, such as women, children, and old people, tend to be identified *by* their association with men, parents, and adult offspring. Here I am speaking of the woman's, child's, and old person's identification *with* the other.

child's success becomes the parents' success because the wife "loves" the husband and the parent "loves" the child. This common-sense notion of "love" holds the spouses and generations together through a largely one-sided identification. This identification averts envy on the part of those who live vicariously— women and old people—by offering a "pseudo-redistribution" of rewards; e.g., honor, recognition. Such vicarious living can make one feel like a "have" when one may not be one; when, in fact, social and economic rewards are not distributed equitably. This pseudo-redistribution of rewards then ensures solidarity in the face of the more disruptive emotion of envy, and the more disruptive behavior of rivalry.

A certain degree of identification with another is probably essential to a deep love relationship in that it allows the individual to share the fortunes and misfortunes of the loved one. However, when identification is not reciprocal and when one party substitutes vicarious living for direct living—as in altruistic surrender—plainly something else is operating, something that passes for "love" but is not essential to it. Urban industrial life calls for the development of autonomy. Juxtaposed with this ideal, altruistic surrender no longer seems like normal "love" but rather seems to be an alternative to autonomy, especially for ascriptive groups, such as old people and women, who are taken out of the running for social rewards. All this does not mean that if women and old people were put back into the competitive arena, if more autonomy were expected of them; social solidarity between men and women, young and old, would decline. It does mean that the nature of the solidarity would be different.

With so few cases it is hard to explore variations in this pattern, but on the basis of these few, it seemed that altruistic surrender was not linked to the degree of current contact with the identified-with. Although Delia was unusually close to her daughter, her identification was typical of the others on her floor. One disengaged woman, Grandma Goodman, saw her son once a month, although her other children in Oklahoma wrote her regularly and saw her on Christmas. Grandma Goodman got up each morning at five o'clock and drank a cup of coffee while lying in bed, looking out her bedroom window until around 9:00. When I asked her what she was thinking about those early morning hours, she replied, surprised at the question, "about my children, of course." In conversations about her children, she focused on her grandson, and his high school graduation, which took place a ten-minute drive away and which she did not attend. Even when kin ties are shorn down to ritualistic occasions and Mother's Day cards, this vicarious "living through" remains.

Altruistic surrender also seemed unlinked to the success or happiness of the person identified with, since in one case a grandmother was carried through the torments of the daughter's divorce and turn to alcohol. Neither did it seem linked to the degree of authority the grandmother had over the identified-with. Although the residents are fairly alike socially, the slight differences in social origin among them also seemed unlinked to the propensity to live vicariously. Furthermore, it did not seem to be linked to the number of children or grandchildren a grandmother had. On the other hand, it was partly linked to the sex of the child or grandchild.

Identification often persisted in the face of important differences between the generations.* Compared to the grand-

---

* For example, the granddaughter of one resident was a student at a junior college, and her concerns centered on her classes in dental nursing, her dates with boyfriends, and her proposed trip with a boyfriend to a folk festival in New York. Her boyfriend, who came to dinner every so often at Merrill Court, had shoulder-length hair and had just returned from a stint with the Army in Vietnam. He opposed the war. As the grandmother, who had made forty ditty bags for the boys in Vietnam, mentioned, after the grandchildren left:

> There's been a lot of changes. The kids don't have to work so hard these days. And you can't get a good job without going to college. I was earning 50 cents a day by the time I was 14, taking in laundry. I'd never . . . thought about college.

Nevertheless, the grandmother called or was called by her granddaughter frequently and followed her life with great interest, as she would a daytime TV drama.

mothers, the daughters' and granddaughter's life cycles have differed, though not drastically. Their childhood has not been so stretched to adult standards of work. Their adolescence was elaborated with a teenage subculture and teenage market, and for many of the granddaughters it has lasted through junior college. Marriage came later (the average age was 21 for daughters), and children were fewer (average 2.6), while other avenues of generativity were at least available. Thus, the biographies of the grandmothers and their daughters reflect different social and historical contexts, but the identification in parental love seems able to transcend these differences.[14]

The quality of the grandmothers' relations to their children is probably not unique to them but is shared with others in similar circumstances. Perhaps all normal people at some time, to some extent, in some relation approximate altruistic surrender. But on the whole, the surrenderers and the surrendered-to are unevenly distributed throughout the population. There are four main conditions that make altruistic surrender more probable.

First, relatively deprived people are more likely to approximate "altruistic surrender" than are the non-deprived. Movie magazines that disclose the "intimate details," "the inside story" of the life of a movie star or of a famous, typically non-deprived political figure provide fodder for identification, and are most popular among the deprived—the poor, the old, women.[15]

Among the relatively deprived we count those whose ambitions surpass the opportunities for fulfilling them.* An example is the automobile worker who aspires to owning his own chicken farm but lacks the capital, the hospital orderly who doesn't have the money for medical school, the stagehand who never trained in acting, the typist who wants to be but never visualized herself as a novelist, the airport guard who failed the pilot training vision test, the dentist who flunked pre-med chemistry, the graduate student who aspires to brilliant work and can't muster the cour-

---

* In Robert Merton's terms, it is those who accept society's goals but lack access to the institutionalized means of attaining them who will be more likely to fit the model. (Merton, 1957.)

age to take his prelims, and the fat teenager who aspires to be slender and cannot stop eating. There are others whose aspirations exceed their real chances for other kinds of reasons—the black girl who wants to enter the Miss Utah contest, the woman who wants to run for the Senate, the old person who wants to continue his work but is forced to retire. Some of these "failings" have more to do with the characteristics of the individual, some more with the characteristics of society.

Second, those who, in addition to the above, are in contact with the potential object of envy are more likely to approximate altruistic surrender. The automobile worker would more likely show symptoms if he worked in a small company directly under a very successful businessman and maintained daily contact with him. In Genet's play *The Maids,** the indistinguishability of the maid and the mistress suggest such a situation. Anna Freud's patient, the governess, is another example. Secretaries who work closely with their bosses, wives who live with their husbands, graduate students who work under professors, fat girls who carry the thin girls' books home every day fill this condition of close contact. There is also a familiar and more impersonal form of altruistic surrender that thrives in spite of distance from a hero. Movie magazines and TV interview shows, for example, make the stars more real, human, and available for identification.

Thus, those persons who have found someone willing or not unwilling to be identified with are more likely to exhibit "altruistic surrender." ** There are many who live life directly and

---

* In his play *The Maids,* Genet captures the interchange of two identities, one that of the maid, Claire, and the other that of her mistress, Solage. "Claire: Be still. It will be your task, yours alone to keep us both alive. You must be very strong. In prison no one will know that I'm with you, secretly. On the sly. I call upon you to represent me. To represent me to the world" (1961, p. 97).

** To test this statement, we would have to find out to what extent the privileged (non-deprived) also live vicariously through the lives of others. Although it is probably a relative matter, I suggest that the young do not "live through" the old *as much* as the old live through the young, that men do not "live through" women *as much* as women live through men, that the mistress does not "live through" the maid *as much* as the maid lives through the mistress.

who are willing to be the "vehicle" of other people's vicarious living. Such a psychological vessel can be local and directly available (for example, a daughter, an employer, a friend) or not directly available (for example, media heroes, movie stars, political figures). Rich, young adult, male whites compose a fairly privileged stratum of the American population and they are a category within which "psychological vessels" can be found. But they fill this role only if the identifiers feel "that could be me."

Fourth, there are organizational and ideological supports for altruistic surrender. The vicariously ambitious wife of a lawyer has the Lawyers' Wives Club, the diplomat's wife has the American women's clubs, and secretaries have the Seraphics Club.* These organizations, built around "vicarious roles," promote a legitimating ideology for altruistic surrender. Ninki Burger's *The Executive's Wife* is a good inside account of the tactics of supporting one's husband's career and the costs and supposed benefits of altruistic surrender. The graduate student's long apprenticeship, or research assistantship, also latently fosters altruistic surrender.

Thus, those persons who meet all four conditions are most likely to show symptoms of altruistic surrender, and the absence of any one condition weakens the probability. In general, it is those who are barred from or fail in competition for scarce rewards but who still covet those rewards who are most susceptible to altruistic surrender. The old are deprived of youth and the social rewards that go with it. They are in close contact with a person who agrees to be identified with. There is also the legitimating ideology of "parental love." If there are no formal organizations that support altruistic surrender, there are also few structures to support alternative life styles. In this respect, Merrill Court is an exception.

I have suggested that the quality of the grandmothers' rela-

---

* Unlike the other clubs, membership in the Seraphics Secretaries of America is based on occupation. However, the executive for whom the secretary works is selected before the secretary is approached to join. If he dies, she must resign. (*New York Times*, December 2, 1968. Also see Hochschild, 1969.)

tions to their children is not unique to them but is shared with other relatively deprived people under conditions of close contact, with proper "vehicles" to identify with, structural support, and legitimating ideology. This suggests that motherly vicarious living, when it becomes a substitute for direct living, is not "innate" in mothers or old people, in their love of others. It is mixed with social deprivation, disguised by the label of "love."

Identification is a matter of degree; any given relationship can fit the model of altruistic surrender closely or only slightly. The process can be personal and direct or impersonal and indirect. It can be culturally sanctioned or not. Finally, the language I have used in describing altruistic surrender suggests that something is wrong with it, that it is like a disease. Some degree of identification with others is part of "real" love and is, I think, an enrichment of life. However, excessive identification with others, which also goes by the name of love, is, I suggest, a response to social deprivation. When low-status people (blacks, women, the old) identify with high-status people (whites, men, the fairly young) they are more likely to accept the distribution of social rewards in the status quo. They identify with the rewarded person instead of seeking those rewards directly themselves. In this way, identification is a means of latent social control and makes the governesses of the world satisfied with remaining underprivileged. If rewards and opportunities were more equally distributed, surrenderers and the surrendered-to would be more evenly distributed throughout the population and its race, class, sex and age groups. Or, everyone would identify and be identified with to a more nearly equal extent.

However, altruistic surrender for the old is in some ways different from what it is for the young. Some deprivations such as the loss of income and honor can be changed or compensated, whereas other deprivations of old age can not. One can not rearrange society so that life is prolonged indefinitely. It seems that there will always be a beginning and an end of it. But this way of handling deprivation remains, whether we call it in some cases a "symptom" or in other cases do not.

The grandmothers of Merrill Court have, in light of this, an added advantage. Their society together offers them not just a chance to share their vicarious lives. It offers an alternative to vicarious living—a chance to live directly, in the here and now, in one's given body whatever its disabilities. Among the "sisters" there is seldom the stable patterned relationship of identifier and identified-with. In the sibling bond it is not, "You do and I'll watch" but rather, "What did you watch?" "I watched this," and, more important, "I'm doing this, what are you doing?" Thus the bonds with kin and with fellow residents perform different emotional functions, which may account for the fact that, in the lives of the grandmothers, kin ties and peer ties are not interchangeable.

chapter six

REFLECTIONS FROM OUTSIDE

The social circle of widows had more than diplomatic ties with the outside world. If the outside world was brought in through television, newspapers, and traveling salesmen, the old also ventured out into the small declining Protestant churches, the crowded waiting rooms in the county hospital, the acres of shopping center nearby, the banks, fraternal organizations, and countywide Senior Citizen Forum.

So far I have tried to show how the old were integrated into the old age subculture and family; now I shall describe how the old age community itself is integrated into the larger society and how various images of the widows are reflected back to them. Through relations—patient to doctor, tenant to housing authority, shopper to clerk—the widows learned what others assume about them, and about *other* old people.

Television: The Heroine's Mother

Perhaps the main way the outside world came to them was through television and newspapers. No apartment at Merrill Court was without a television* and almost all residents watched it regularly. Only one, who was a member of the Pentecostal church, refused to watch on moral principle because, as she explained, the indoor antennas were the two horns of the Devil.) In most apartments TV provided some friendly noise, some automated company. Often the women looked at it intermittently, while chatting with a friend, or fixing a meal, just to keep in touch with a plot development or to join in the applause of an audience participation show.

Several programs engrossed them, among them the daytime serials, "Love of Life," "Search for Tomorrow," "As the World Turns," "General Hospital," "Love Is a Many Splendored Thing," "Guiding Light," "Edge of Night," and "One Life to Live." Next in popularity were game and other audience participation programs and after that cowboy programs such as "Gunsmoke." ** Three women expressed regret that the Monday morning club

---

* The widows were fairly typical of widows and single women over 60 in the general population. According to Beyer and Woods, nine out of ten widowed or single women over 60 (living with others) own a TV and about eight out of ten living alone do. Of those who own TV's, about eight out of ten watch it regularly (Beyer and Woods, 1963, pp. 13–14; Meyersohn, 1961).

** Most were specifically not interested in murder mysteries. Older viewers like audience participation programs such as "This Is Your Life," "Strike it Rich," "People Are Funny," "Truth or Consequences," and "Queen for a Day." Such programs feature everyday people playing important roles. (Meyersohn, 1961.)

meeting was scheduled at 10:00 o'clock because it conflicted with "General Hospital."

In some ways the message, not the media, was the message. Although we know something about how children react to television,[1] we know next to nothing about what the programs they watch mean to old people, and especially to old women. Take for example, "As the World Turns." One important minor character in it is the grandmother, played by an actress who looks about 40 or 45, is only a tiny bit overweight, well dressed, and has smoothly coiffured hair. (The grandfather, a retired lawyer, on the other hand, looks about 60 to 65 and is dressed slightly less formally. His occupation is not strategic to the plot and the only suggestion of it is the affluent living room and bedroom in which the scene is set. Thus, the TV grandmother, unlike the real grandmothers, was not old, was not widowed, and was not poor.

The TV grandmother was sympathetic, "understanding," and a person of indirect influence. People came to her in helplessness to ask her to exert influence: "Talk to her, I can't make her understand." She manipulated behind the scenes rather than directly interfering in her daughter's life. For example, she called her daughter to report on the activities of the daughter's former husband. She paid a visit to her daughter's former husband, a doctor, at the strategic moment—when he was seeing another woman. But her advice was frequently disobeyed, ignored, or was shown, in light of other information, to be irrelevant. A scene frequently ended with a tremorous minor chord from the organ, the grandmother's facial expression suggesting worry or incomprehension that was not followed up by action.

When at one point the heroine daughter impetuously left town against her mother's advice, the grandmother took care of the grandchild, who was himself a fund of information upon which the plot unfolded. The grandmother was thus a social cushion to each divorce, taking in the grandchild and freeing the daughter for yet another round of mate selection. She was also the child's watchdog, reluctantly preventing the imploring former husband from seeing his son. Thus it was a traditionally female world, and, within it, the significance and power of women was magnified; the grandfather was but a diminished version of the grandmother. Although he was, in contrast to the young suitors, more expressive than instrumental, it was mainly the "human" side of everyone's life that was portrayed, even in the office.

But both grandparents were subordinate to the young daughter and her (usually former) husband whose doings and undoings of love and marriage were central to the drama. In almost all nine daytime dramas there was either a killing, adultery, or an illegitimate child. (In fact, one widow suggested, "All them stories, they're written by the same fella.") These events happened to and were done by the *young* adults and were important to the grandparents only insofar as they affected their children.

The widows talked over the plot developments almost every day. When one had to miss a program for a doctor's appointment, another reported on it for her, so that she did not lose her place in the serial. In this talk, however, they seldom mentioned the grandmother, and there were more "If I were her . . ." remarks about the young heroine than about her older mother. The TV grandmother was not the sort of person one does identify with, since she was portrayed as having few interests in life other than her daughter and her problems; she was the very model of altruistic surrender. But it does not seem to be a double altruistic surrender; that is, real grandmothers identifying with fictional grandmothers who, in turn, identify with heroine-daughters. Rather, the grandmothers put themselves directly in the place of the daughter herself. The program offered a model of altruistic surrender as well as a pseudo reflection of it.

The drama stressed the vertical ties between the older generation and the younger to the exclusion of horizontal ties with age peers. Outside of the family, the older characters did not know one another. Although they were each independently interested in the goings-on of the younger generation, they had no solidarity among themselves faintly resembling that at Merrill Court. The younger hero and heroine did have age peers in their neighbors and friends, who, like the grandmother, helped from the sidelines in time of crisis, which was most of the time. But the older characters did not.

The glamour, youth, and affluence of the television lives appealed to the grandmothers in ways in which they appeal to all viewers, especially people deprived of just those things. The essence of glamour, as I suggested earlier, is the beauty of youth combined with the wealth and fame of middle age. The grandmothers, having neither youth nor wealth and fame, are the opposite of glamorous. They do not measure up even to the TV grandmother, who, although luckier, wealthier, and younger than they, altruistically surrenders to the glamorous young heroine.

Newspapers

The outside world also filtered in through newspapers. Most of the residents subscribed to the weekly *Verada News.** This weekly was not actually a "news" paper, since it did not print information that was new within the last day, or even information that most regular subscribers already had received from TV and radio. Since the weekly paper had only two reporters, most of its stories were based on news releases from the local government, chamber of commerce, and voluntary organizations.

I did a content analysis on every third issue of the 104 copies of the *Verada News* from June 30, 1967 to July 19, 1969.** Initially, I thought that old people would be greatly under-represented in the community press in proportion to their number in the population. As it turned out, this was not the case. About 19 percent of the population of the county were over 65 and

---

* In the general population, 45 percent of those over 65 read newspapers every day (Steiner, 1963, pp. 344, 347) and over half of the Merrill Court grandmothers do.

** The *Verada News* has a circulation of 10,000 and comes out once a week. Each issue has from four to eight pages with an average of 50 to 100 news items.

about 12 percent of all news items with photographs attached portrayed people over 65. Middle-aged people were over-represented and children were under-represented.

The community newspaper, unlike the metropolitan dailies, did not primarily report acts of deviance;[2] only 18 percent of the news items dealt with local crime, arrests, and trials. Another 10 percent of the news items dealt with other kinds of deviance or unusual events, such as the drowning of a fisherman, a brush fire, or injury to a bicyclist. One story told of some junior college student archeologists who discovered an Indian burial ground in a new apartment construction site.* (The apartment went up anyway. Even the ancient dead apparently were not honored over commercial interests.)

The 12 percent of news items that focused on old people usually reported a birthday celebration, typically an 80th or 90th, or a golden or silver wedding anniversary. In these cases, age itself was the "deviant" or unusual point of interest. Other items on older people stressed their activities. For example, one story had a photograph of an 80-year-old woman active in the Cancer Society. She was pictured standing with a pencil in her hand and phone to her ear.

To the grandmothers, the very reporting of an event *was* the news. The women would call one another up, not to tell about who received the bowling trophy—which they knew soon after it

---

* The other two-thirds of the items dealt with the non-deviant side of life. Many such items told of what had not yet happened: "The Verada Eagles and Auxiliary *will be busy* . . . both *will* attend a whist party in the local hall . . . a gun-handling class of the Junior Rifle Club will begin." Some non-news items also reported what was currently happening: "Engineer-Manager Notes That Sanitary District Budget Is Being Studied."

The most common kind of item reported a change in status, and the rite of passage linked with it, such as a marriage, appointment, promotion, retirement, special honors or assignments, and death. For example, *A* succeeded *B* as president of the Lion's Club, initiation of class candidates to the Fraternal Order of Eagles by the state president, two young men enlisted in the navy, a man retired from the Chamber of Commerce, a man received a bowling trophy, or a woman received the blue ribbon in the flower show.

happened—but to relate that the event had been reported in the newspaper. For example, Irma entered the recreation room one morning saying, "Did you see that Neda had her picture in the paper this week? It was a nice photo. I wonder if her daughter saw it." The reporting of what was old news seemed to sanctify it by making an informally public event a formally public one.

In two years there were nine news items with photographs of one or several residents of Merrill Court. Typically they focused on "good works" such as the ditty bags made for the boys in Vietnam, the trips to entertain people in the nursing homes, and the cards cut for muscular dystrophy. In addition to these nine items was a five- or six-line weekly notice announcing coming events such as the weekly card or bingo game, the potluck luncheon or dinner, or bowling. Although the widows knew very well what events were coming, they nevertheless read the news items faithfully, noting to whom credit was given and not given. The annual group photograph of newly installed officers was clipped out and pinned to the bulletin board for all to see.

It was their formal life downstairs, not their informal life upstairs, their public not their private life, their association with other old people, not with younger family, that was reflected back to them by the press. Activity tended to earn them public visibility, inactivity earned them invisibility. And if television showed vertical ties to the young, newspapers reflected horizontal ties to age peers.

The Commercial World

The outside world came to Merrill Court in other ways too, refracting an image of old people in yet a different light. By looking at their relations in the commercial world I hope to show how others treated them and how they reduced impersonality and coped with exploitation. As mentioned before, people came to the building to sell things. Typically, a middle-aged cosmetic saleslady arranged for a demonstration of her wares at one of the

Monday morning business meetings of the Service Club. She described the merits of various facial creams, powders, and lipstick, and the women drank coffee and commented on the wares. On one occasion, when a $9 jar of "Eterna" facial cream was held up, one woman remarked, to an approving group, "That stuff ain't gonna help my wrinkles none. I used a good cake of soap all my life. I don't spose this stuff'll help me now." Although the pensioners were not a good market for the high-priced items, there were usually three or four sales of perfume or lipstick for Christmas gifts to female relatives.

Demonstrators also brought in arts and crafts, kitchen utensils, and food. One popular salad chopper was bought wholesale by the club and distributed to the group at a low price. Luncheons furnished by the Ladies League Auxiliary, advertised to the public in the newspaper, provided food companies with free advertising, and the widows with a free lunch. As one widow later described it, "Oh, they tried to sell us food. They want to get our pension checks, I guess. Suppose they think somethin's in 'em."

On other occasions free-lance salesmen came around. One woman, who lived in the same trailer park as the Recreation Leader, went door to door in the apartment house selling homemade rain hats at $2.50 each. ("$1.50 for labor, I figure that's fair.") And one resident went door to door selling knitted socks just before Christmas in order to earn bus fare for a trip home.

The women exchanged tales about how they had been "taken in" by or had outsmarted peddlers, mainly magazine salesmen. One Oklahoman reported:

> I tell them I can't read or write. I just told the man that I was born in the mountains and didn't go to the country school. He left pretty fast. He couldn't sell me a magazine I couldn't read.*

* There were many such stories of "playing dumb." One woman recounted how she got her first job in California: "I went to the cannery and the man asked how many children I had. I told him I had six and he said I should stay home with them. What's the use of staying home with them if I can't feed them? But I showed up like regular

Another woman said she always used the "I'm deaf and dumb" ploy. A third never opened the door without a chain across it when it looked like a peddler at the door. Others confessed buying from peddlers and regretting it.

The widows also ventured out into the commercial world, either collectively or singly, often personalizing relations as they went. The Service Club, for example, held an annual bake sale at the nearby shopping plaza. Before the event a delegation from Merrill Court visited the local store manager to arrange about setting up tables. Since his cooperation was taken as a personal gesture, they always responded in kind by offering him a free cake. Other club affairs sent a delegation of widows into the outside world for wholesale supplies, to get free day-old doughnuts, to arrange for a free monthly birthday cake from a nearby bakery, or to arrange for luncheons at the bowling alley. On each occasion the delegation introduced themselves by name and as "the Merrill Court Senior Citizens Club." As these connections with the lower and middle management of local enterprises became routinized, the widows got to know the names of the managers they dealt with regularly. The managers, on the other hand, seldom recalled their names and referred to them rather as "you ladies" or "you folks over there."

Very often their children provided a link with the surrounding commercial world and a store checker or sales clerk or hairdresser might be referred to as "Hattie's sister's boy" or "Alma's daughter-in-law." The bake sale mentioned above was at "the store where Ernestine's son works," and the son was introduced around to the widows at the bake sale table. Often a child was a source of information, a personal woodworm within the large impersonal bureaucracy whose policies touched their lives. For example, Delia's daughter worked for the Social Security Administration putting social security numbers and information on

---

for work the next day and I told them I worked there regular but had been off a week tending my sick child. He gave me a time card and I worked there 20 years. I ain't no dumb Okie."

tape. On request, she would look up the number of a person on social security and report how much he received. Another daughter worked in the housing authority. Since they pooled information from such sources and shared one another's social contacts, the widows seldom ventured out without meeting someone who was "known." * Although changes in such things as the food stamp policy, or social security, or Medicare coverage appeared to come from "on high," the ranks of those who administered these policies on the local level were interpenetrated by "known" people.

Even in the daytime, shopping** was hazardous for the old women. From 1965 to 1968 five purses in the building were stolen. The nearer to Merrill Court the incident happened, the more talk there was about it. On one occasion, Milly returned to the recreation room from a shopping trip, reporting a stolen wallet.

> I was standing at the bus stop, and I had my purse clutched right under my arm but my wallet was in my hand. I was taking out bus fare. It was a young boy. He just snatched my wallet away and ran. It's merciful I just had the 25 cents in it.

Two widows were robbed of their entire monthly pensions on their way home from the bank.

On all such occasions the widows held emergency meetings to decide what to do. After one robbery a delegation from Mer-

---

* One woman who arranged for the delivery of the monthly free birthday cake from a local bakery knew three generations of the bakery's ownership. "I went in to see the young fellow who's taken over the business now. I told him I knowed his dad and his mother and his aunt and his father's stepdad. He was friendly to me. They started on a shoestring, you know. Must be millionaires now."
** Many devoted an entire shopping trip to the search for one low-cost item, such as a spool of thread or a birthday card. They shopped mainly at nearby stores, and became selective shoppers, drawing the best bargains from more distant stores only when they could find someone to drive them. It was often while they shopped that they were reminded of bygone friends or relatives. "Whenever I see a game-hen at the Safeway, I think of Little Floyd. I used to think, 'I'll get Little Floyd a hen for dinner.' "

rill Court went to the store manager of the nearby shopping center to ask for protection, which they failed to get. After each theft, a person was appointed to go around to all residents taxing them to reimburse the victim. The money was slipped under the person's door later. This custom served the function of an insurance company, like the early Friendly Societies of the English working class.[3]

After news of the robbery spread through the building, conversations would turn to the dangers of the encroaching black population of the neighboring city, and to the lawlessnes of modern-day youth.* The women noted that the robber was usually a young Negro adolescent under the tutelage of an older one, and blame was usually pinned on the older adolescent and then on his parents, or the Negro race. Nearby there was a black ghetto with a high unemployment rate, over-crowded schools, and *de facto* segregated housing. Thus, the widows were victimized by another category of social victims, as is often the case.[4] Most of these white, rural born, working-class residents revealed prejudice against blacks even in the arguments they gave for their lack of it.** Anti-black feeling became overt one summer when there were a number of racial incidents. The widows became frightened, locked their doors during the day, and some left to live with children for a week. As one explained, "You can't tell what

---

* On the other hand, young people often see the elderly as opposed to their recreation and way of life. In an article "But Would You Want One to Move Next Door?" by Kyle Given, a "little old lady" was portrayed in a rocking chair in the middle of the road, presumably an obstacle to car racers. (*Car and Driver*, October, 1969.)

** My first year there, five widows confided to me that they personally thought Negroes were "just as good as" white folks, but that a lot of others here didn't think so. Their own prejudice came out in the supporting argument for their lack of prejudice. "Some of them works hard. We knew a fella, kep' his house up real nice. We moved out of that neighborhood, though. Got to be too many, you know." Or in another case, one widow commented, "I like them, they're real friendly, some of them at the church. We do a lot for 'em. I gave this one lady some clothes. She 'preciated that."

might happen. They may come and burn the buildin' down. I'm takin' my photograph album with me."

In none of the instances of purse stealing were the police called, and they too came in for criticism. It was generally felt that the police were a necessary agency in the community but that they "get paid for sittin', and usin' up gas in their cars to get their wives free stamps." * In many cases, they knew the police from encounters with their grandsons; "They're too hard on the young boys, they get them to confess and then give them a stiff sentence. It isn't fair. But I don't know where we'd be without the police, the world goin' the way it is."

Whether the outside commercial world came to them or they went to it, they saw themselves as something of an economic market although not much of one, as those indistinguishable "ladies over there," and as helpless victims of petty crime. They coped with the commercial world by personalizing it and if they identified a store clerk as somebody's daughter or granddaughter, they were in turn recognized as someone's grandmother or mother. Most of the grocery checkers, saleswomen, bank tellers, and waitresses with whom they dealt were young, and the widows were a minority among them. They remarked among themselves about comments or facial expressions from other shoppers if they moved their carts too slowly in the shopping line, or took longer to pay for a purchase.

Although the women turned commercial relations into personal ones, and made shopping into a recreation,** they did not overly personalize commercial relations and shopping was seldom a way of relieving loneliness. No residents fit the description of the lonely older person who whiles away the time of a

---

* Many policemen bought gasoline at gas stations that gave out green stamps that were refundable at green stamp stores.
** They seldom passed a wig counter in the five-and-ten-cent store without joking about the thought of what they would look like in a red or blonde wig. On one occasion, a group of four tried on the wigs, as if to revisit youth with the distance of humor.

busy bank clerk described, from the point of view of a bank trust officer, below:

> The bank . . . is doing all that is legally required of it as trustee . . . it is giving good management to the financial assets, accounting for its stewardship and seeing that a proper amount of money is used for, or made available to, the person. In fact, the bank is going beyond its duty . . . by permitting Mrs. Jones to consume an inordinate amount of the trust officer's time. She relieves her loneliness by visiting him once every week or two and staying for perhaps thirty minutes to chat. This becomes a problem from the bank's point of view. It points up one of the inherent shortcomings of the system of fiduciary relationships. . . ." [5]

If the widows occasionally had to be protected when they ventured into the commercial world, the commercial world did not have to be protected from them, or from the demands on time and resources that lonely old people make.

Senior Citizens in a Welfare State

If the widows were a market to the commercial world, they were an object of welfare to the recreation department, social welfare department, and housing authority. If they were white-haired ladies who moved too slowly in a department store, they were "senior citizens" in the eyes of the Recreation Leader, the welfare worker, and the housing authority officials. In this section I will try to show how the widows coped with and felt about the lower officials who linked them to the mountainous welfare bureaucracy that ministers to the needs of the old. It is this administrative world, dealing with people as they fit age categories, that reinforces the age-stratification in the society at large, mentioned in Chapter Two.

All but two had never heard of the term "senior citizen" before coming to California and their age peers back East, whom they visited yearly, seldom went by that name. It was only on occasion, as when they showed their senior citizen cards to get medicine from the druggist, to qualify for Medicare benefits, that they became senior citizens in the commercial world. They generally liked the term "senior citizens" and, like the Recreation Director, referred to themselves as "seniors."

Most were grateful for the low rent and the new apartment, and the work supplies of paint, paper, brushes, and yarn provided by the Recreation and Parks Department; but they felt no need of *social* aid. Their financial aid, as they saw it, came from an impersonal source. Many were quite willing to accept impersonal aid but firmly avoided accepting personal aid. As one widow commented, "I don't accept gifts from anyone. I wouldn't have anyone take in my sewing and sew me a dress without paying her. No, sir. I never have." Yet in another context, she was strongly opposed to the California Governor's proposal to cut welfare benefits. When aid came through impersonal channels, no one in particular deserved their gratitude. The bank clerks from whom they collected their monthly checks were not seen as providers or donors. It was rather an amorphous abstraction called the state to which they owed thanks.

Among themselves they were equals, and they gave as much as they took. *Other* people outside the community saw them as welfare recipients, beneficiaries of good works and charity, other people's "poor dears," and they felt the stigma of that. One widow expressed it:

> They (the Recreation and Parks Department) think we're all senile here, can't take care of ourselves. There isn't a one of us here who can't. But that's what J . . . thinks, those poor seniors over there. He comes to our Christmas party and he thinks he's doin' us a big favor.*

* There was actually only one person who was senile in Merrill Court, and he was in, but not of, the community. This suggests what other research has shown, that senility is to a large extent socially constructed. One study of post mortem biopsies of supposedly senile old people showed no physical brain deterioration. Social isolation may well produce the senile behavior. This may account for its absence in Merrill Court.

A few harbored similar suspicions about the welfare workers who dropped in to visit them, and the housing authority officials to whom they paid the monthly rent and complained about a leaking roof or a draft coming from a crack under the door.

Most of the lower-level personnel in the welfare and housing bureaucracies who deal with the old directly are middle-aged women. As these agencies take over the former functions of the family in providing for the elderly, their personnel are sociological daughters, "helping mother out." But, increasingly, professional men are moving into these jobs, thus simulating a family pattern of the nineteenth century when it was more often the son than the daughter who took in an aging parent.[6]

These immediate links are, in any case, only part of an intricate maze of relations linking the widows to the broader welfare state. The network itself lends structural support to the growing stratification by age. The Older American Act, passed by Congress in 1965, is important mainly because it authorizes federal money to state governments, which can in turn finance county and city projects, both public and private non-profit. The Federal Commission on Aging has nine regional offices, one in San Francisco. California has, in addition, the California Commission on Aging, a state agency (since 1955), and it maintains contact with the federal regional office in San Francisco. The state Commission on Aging, along with the state Recreation and Parks Department, has links to the county level. The county, in turn, maintains links with the city or town. The head of the city Recreation and Parks Department has, in turn, two people working under him, one a parks supervisor and the other a recreation supervisor. It is the recreation supervisor of Verada who hires recreation directors who work in particular senior citizen clubs.

About fifty senior citizens clubs are chartered with the State Commission on Aging and some clubs exist that are not chartered.* Not all chartered clubs draw old people from public

---

* Only an estimated 10 percent of those 65 and over are active in senior citizen clubs in the county. Most of the sixty or so delegates

housing projects. This county has, since 1969, had eighteen senior citizens clubs and club representatives gather once a month for a Senior Citizen Forum.

In the minds of the widows, the administrative links at the federal and state levels remain vague and undifferentiated. They know that "something's going on for old people" on a national level, but they link it to the actions of the President and not the National Commission on Aging. On the local level it is a different matter. Over the last year, ten members have gone to one of the monthly meetings of the Senior Citizen Forum. News spread rapidly about what was going on at the other senior centers nearby. One delegation reported on a young male Recreation Director who worked with thirty-five elderly widows (his "harem," as he called them) and a 98-year-old club chairman. Forum delegates also returned with news on such topics as a new transportation project by which senior citizens pay a dollar a month to travel anywhere in the vicinity by bus, Medicare benefits, talks by nutritional experts, club blood banks, sight-saver books (books in larger print), the recruiting of new members by going through church registers, and Older Americans Month—May.

There were fairly strong lateral ties to other old age housing projects and senior citizen drop-in centers. Once when Merrill Court was plagued by factional disputes, several residents warned that word had spread to a nearby senior citizen project about "talks and fightin' goin' on over here." A number were regulars

---

who turned up at the monthly meetings were retired, small-business men. In the speeches by the three primary officers of the Forum, there was a stress on "salesmanship." The secretary of the Forum commented, "I stop people in the store and tell them about the next senior citizen meeting. We have to sell this idea to people. We have to get the idea across, see." He and a number of others also suggested having an "early sixties" club, distinct from other clubs, to win new recruits, since those in the early sixties were (and are) the most reluctant to join. It was also suggested to have a "men only" club to recruit men who were afraid of being overwhelmed with the female company of other senior citizen clubs. There is a club of retired businessmen called "Sirs." (It stands for Seniors in Retirement.)

at old age groups such as "Let's Dance" and "The Forty-Niners," and those who did not belong to "The Golden Agers" had friends who did.*

The widows were suspicious of those who had authority over them, and that meant those in the mountainous bureaucracy that deal with old age. The chief of the Recreation and Parks was known as a man who lived up "in the hills" and estimates of his annual salary were much exaggerated. He came to the annual Christmas party and installation of club officers, but, as the widows noticed, he seldom brought his wife and normally left soon after a brief speech (which usually included a joke about his balding head and the prospects of joining the senior citizens). Since they did not feel known by him, they suspected his motives and exaggerated his powers. For example, in the issue mentioned earlier, whether to keep the $900 club funds under the Treasurer's bed or in the bank, the widows feared that the Recreation and Park Director would himself steal the hard-earned money, if the bank did not. Again, they thought the building contractor for Merrill Court was "up to no good," although the mayor (and friend of the contractor), who occasionally dropped over to play his saxophone, was not suspect.

Those unknown were generally distrusted and those who were known, whether they were liked or disliked,[6] were generally trusted.** As Georg Simmel pointed out, trust of an individual

---

* The Golden Agers was described by one regular member. "They play games, everything except cards. After the meeting they go to a chapel for a devotional. They don't use bad language. They're Christian people. You get three free trips a year and three free dinners a month. It's ten cents a week."

** But those known to the community are not generally distrusted. When a pound of butter was found missing from the refrigerator downstairs, people knew who took it and they privately condemned her for the act. They did not, however, maintain a general attitude of doubt toward everyone or even the guilty party. Their suspicions were confined to "butter-snitching." The same pattern developed in response to a woman who cheated on her bowling scores. For an analysis of distrust, see Wolff, 1950; for a discussion of distrust in the working class, see Archibald, 1947; Shostag and Gomberg, 1964; and Knupfer, 1953.

can be the functional equivalent of knowledge of that individual. If we have to deal with a person we do not know, we must usually make some assumptions on trust. The widows seemed to lack such trust, and this may be because they knew little about the public and legal arrangements that generally force people to be honest. The widows might have been more prone to trust the Recreation and Parks chief had they known about bank policy on bank accounts, and transfer of funds, the job of auditors, and the latent functions of secretaries. If one is not versed in the institutional safeguards against dishonesty, it is perhaps safer to assume that unknown people are untrustworthy, which is what the widows did. In some cases, they were probably right—the building was, in fact, sloppily constructed and each rain would bring new complaints about mildewed rugs; but I do not have enough information to know whether or not they were wise to distrust all the authorities as much as they did.

Closer to home, the widows saw images of themselves through the two successive recreation leaders, the most "indigenous" representatives of the welfare state. Both were well known to the widows and they were not distrusted, although one was generally liked and the other hated. The recreation directors are worth discussing because the widows' reaction to them says a good deal about the widows themselves. The first recreation leader, Ruby, was a popular middle-aged former waitress, dancer, and comedienne. In the mini-state of Merrill Court she functioned as a ward boss, who had connections and protected her own. She was praised for getting ringside seats for the group at the Ice Follies, for getting a restaurant to donate an old dishwarmer to the project, and she was generally described as a "promoter."

Ruby talked much of the time about her financial situation, which was better than theirs. She discussed her tailor-made clothes, the cost of her new Buick, the price of her housekeeper, the number of times she dined out each week, and her son's intellectual success at a local junior college. In her absence, the widows compared her apparent affluence to their own near poverty, but by their tone of voice and content of the remarks, it seemed that they did not feel personally threatened by such remarks.

This stood in contrast to their reaction to the second recreation leader. Kate, a middle-aged divorcee who lived in a trailer, had worked as a typesetter all her life, and talked about money in a different way, since she, like the widows, had less of it. She talked more about age, but in indirect ways. Her choice of words suggested to me, and apparently to them, a prejudice against old people. She usually referred to the widows as "you people," and not, as Ruby did, to "us." Often there was the adjective "little" in front of words like "job," "activity," "apartment," "games," and "seniors." She stressed the active rather than the useful side of the clubs projects; "That should keep you little ladies busy for a while." When she spoke to me alone, this became clearer. Like others with age prejudice, Kate attributed any unusual or unpleasant behavior to being old; "Minnie's so selfish. They get that way when they get old." Also, her praise often reflected low expectations; "She's an alert little lady for someone her age"— much as the statement, "Kids that age are so smart," reflects the fundamental assumption that they are stupid.

About two months after Kate had replaced Ruby, the major social crisis of the three years I was there occurred. Kate had remarked that welfare policies were arranged so as to financially punish the widow who remarried, in that single men and women earn collectively more in payments than a married couple. By the afternoon of the next day, word was around that Kate had said that senior citizens slept with one another without being married. By that evening, word had it that Kate had said that Merrill Court was a house of prostitution. The next day Kate was publicly accused, and one widow burst out, "I can't wait till *you're* old!" Kate was 59. They asked her to resign but she refused. The Recreation and Parks Director came to her support, only confirming their previous suspicion of him. She stayed.

Both leaders kept, however unintentionally, a social distance from the widows. In the first case it was a class difference, in the second, a not-so-large age difference. The aspersions indirectly cast on their relative poverty did not strike a reaction in the community, perhaps because of their identification with their more prosperous children. But this identification could not assuage unkind remarks about age. The widows themselves referred to other old people in derogatory terms, but among their own, such remarks put them up in the hierarchy of "poor dears." As their vehement response suggests, when such remarks came from a younger woman and self-defined outsider, age turned out to be a tender subject.

Children of God

In the vicinity of Merrill Court, peppered between the doggy diners, gas stations, and billboards, are many tiny churches, mostly marginal offshoots of the major Protestant denominations; for example, the Full Gospel Deliverance Center Church, the Powerhouse Church of God in Christ, Pentecostal Holiness Church, and a number of Southern Baptist churches that a number of the widows attended. In an attempt to forestall a decline in the already dwindling coffers, the ministers never tired of stressing that the *young* are the strength of the church.

Although many listened to church music on the radio Sunday mornings and prayed privately, only twelve were regular churchgoers.* The non-goers often expressed admiration for the churchgoers, but made the perennial distinction between being "religious" and "church going." But even those who didn't go to church saw the landscape in terms of distance between churches. Whenever they went on trips they would point out, "That's the

---

* Only one woman in the building was adamantly opposed to church. Born on a Missouri farm, Emma Fieldstone mentioned that she had once been a regular church-goer, but had stopped attending. "No church for me. I quit church. When I was in Oklahoma there was oil found on the land. Some folks had oil on their land and some folks didn't. We didn't. And you go into church and some lady would cock her head and ask, 'How much did you pay for that dress?' I quit church that day."

road to Millie's church" or "Katherine's church is up that way."
Of the twelve church-goers, five went together to the nearby
Baptist church, helping out at revivals and the two-week summer
camp for 150 Baptist children. One widow came into the church
through such service work: "I used to go to church when my kids
were young, to help out. I figured it was my duty. But then I
stopped when they grew up. Now my grandchildren go, and I
figure I should help out again." This church also held a Bible
study class in the Recreation Room of Merrill Court. Its min-
ister, Brother Ken, paid visits to the recently bereaved, gave sermons at funerals, and his choir sang carols for the widows at
Christmas.

The faithful often commented that they felt uplifted after
one of Brother Ken's sermons. The basic theme of his sermons
was that all people of whatever age are small, helpless, and dependent children in the eyes of God. They are born, grow up,
and die as children of God. Among the believers, the widows
are the farthest away from actual childhood. Their own parents
are gone. When they pray, it is usually first for their children
and grandchildren, and only second for their own parents' souls.
One woman remarked, "I always pray for my children first. Then
if I fall asleep before I finish, I know I won't be worried the next
morning."

Most young people, husbands and wives and children, have
living people on whom they can feel dependent; it is especially
for the parentless, spouseless old that the church provides a pallia-
tive in the "father who watches us all." In every society most old
people no longer have living parents, but various societies handle
the fact differently. For example, Mannoni, in *Prospero and
Caliban: The Psychology of Colonization,* analyzed the cult of the
dead in Malagasy society. There, he pointed out, all power is
felt to come from the dead ancestors; all adults are thought to be
the children of the dead. Through belief, the deceased parents
are "kept alive." However, the same transference of adulthood
to "elsewhere" occurs in Western religion where God is, like the
dead for the Malagasy, the all-powerful adult on whom all can

depend.* When there is no living parent and no ideological equivalent on which to legitimately pin feelings of dependency, the feelings remain but are unsanctioned. For the twelve devout members of the community, part of a diminishing enclave in an increasingly secular society, perhaps the church functions to legitimate feelings of dependency that might otherwise find no ideological support.

The Funeral Parlor

The strong loyalty the widows feel toward church and clergy contrasts sharply with their instrumental attitude toward funeral parlors and their young men, dressed in dark suits, who look remarkably like pastors. Indeed, the printed funeral invitations, with an ad for the funeral home and ambulance service on the back, remind the widows that God has less to do with funeral homes than Caesar.

A funeral parlor, unlike a church, is thus judged by how much it charges for a burial and how well the morticians prepare the body. The widows often remarked on how the body looked when it was on view in the coffin: "They curled her hair too tight and tinted it too much. She never tinted her hair." The funeral parlor personnel sometimes had to go by outdated photographs of the deceased to guide them in dressing up the body, and this was a reminder that the personnel had not known the deceased.

The women often compared the various funeral parlors, not only for how they "did a person up" but for the kind of music that was taped through the speakers, the thickness of the rug on

---

* Early American religious writings suggest this image: see William Cooper, *Man Humbled By Being Compar'd to a Worm*, Boston, 1732. As Mannoni points out, dependence relationships contain ". . . no element of comparison or self appraisal, no effort to situate oneself otherwise than within that specific order of things which is the system of dependence" (p. 83). In the sibling relations of the peer community, on the other hand, there is a great deal of comparison and attempts to situate oneself differently.

the chapel floor, and the floral decorations on the side. If the dead person had few friends and few flowers had been sent on behalf of the deceased, the funeral parlor provided plastic flowers and this was considered a "sad thing."

Although various funeral parlors were known to be better than others, it hinged less on the people involved than on the cost. The widows knew no one equivalent to Brother Ken, and their relations with the men in the dark suits were fraught with suspicion, since they expected to be talked into a more expensive funeral than they could afford. Although they knew money was not the measure of devotion, they knew also that others, like funeral directors, thought it was; and since they themselves wanted a dignified end, they felt they owed others the same.

The Doctor's Patient

If the church ministered to the soul and the funeral parlor to the bereaved, the hospital ministered to the bodies of the living. Although most of the residents were in fairly good health and only a few had ailments that prevented them from living an active life, most made a visit to the county hospital's outpatient clinic about once a month.

The role of patient at any age often involves a childlike dependency on the ministrations of the doctor. The old go to the doctor more than the young do and so more often are put in a passive, dependent role. The childlike role of patient, unlike the role of believer, is generally involuntary.

The county hospital is large and specialized, and in the course of one visit a patient may deal with two or three nurses, a physical therapist, a pharmacist, and an x-ray technician, as well as the doctor. In spite of the impersonality, the grandmothers carved out a known portion of the hospital for themselves; they knew the outpatient waiting room, the visiting hours, and the floor of the hospital where a friend stayed during her last visit. One favorite TV program, "General Hospital," portrays the doctor as a man who not only knew his patient, but who was in love with her, as well as with the hospital receptionist. The whole hospital was riddled with love and intrigue. The viewer was given a picture of the personal life behind the occupational one, and of the discrepancy between the two. Maybe one reason why "General Hospital" was a favorite program was its sharp contrast to their own experience in hospitals. They often did not know the doctor nor were they known to him. The professional kindness of the nurses suggested none of the glamour or dramatic raw emotion of the TV program. And on "General Hospital" people rarely died.

Most Merrill Court residents felt that doctors cared less about old patients than young ones. As Irma said, "I was over at County Hospital about a week. They don't care nothin' for ya over there. You're a piece a old meat." Such complaints were common in Merrill Court but, again, they never showed up on the TV program.

Marginal People

Whether the outside world came in to them or they went out to it, it provided the widows with a set of images of themselves and "the old person" as a potential market, as potential victims, as non-people ("you ladies over there"), as senior citizens, as children of God, as the doctor's less-valued patient, as people of whom little is expected ("Isn't it grand how active you people keep."), and as essentially useless ("That should keep you little ladies busy for a while."). Each situational identity, each picture others had of them, added a new dimension to the widows' own self-image.

It is the old more than the young who are most likely to feel the sting of a subtly denigrating remark. And it is the old who are more aware of age itself. Just as the short person is more likely to be aware of height, the marginal student more likely to be conscious of grades, the black to be aware of color differences, so it is the old person who is more likely to be aware of age, and the meaning given it. Isolated or community-less old people, who rely for emotional sustenance on chance encounters with bank clerks and nurses, are probably less protected against denigration and they probably feel it more.*

The communal life of Merrill Court, on the other hand, allows the widows some measure of dignity. If the sum of the widows' contacts outside the peer community suggests that they are not equal to young people, they are on an equal footing with their fellow residents. Inside an old age community one is not entirely insulated from the climate of opinion that prevails in the society at large. But such a community can respond collectively to problems that would be far more serious if faced alone.

* The widows, insulated by a community of peers, feel the sting of stigma less than most isolated older people. Barron notes that ". . . old people react to the stigma of age with self-consciousness, self hatred, and defensiveness which characterize other minority ethnic groups." They generally avoid the label "old." One study showed that compared to most people their age, 65 percent of 500 respondents said they felt younger than others their age (Kutner *et al.*, 1956, pp. 94, 98). Studies using the semantic differential find both old and young to have negative evaluations of old age (Kogan and Wallach, 1961, pp. 277–278; Eisdorfer and Altrocchi, 1962).

EPILOGUE

Old friends
Winter companions
The old men
Lost in their overcoats
Waiting for the sunset
The sounds of the city,
Sifting through trees
Settle like dust
On the shoulders of the old friends.

The most important point I am trying to make in this book concerns the people it does not discuss—the isolated. Merrill Court was an unexpected community, an exception. Living in ordinary apartments and houses, in shabby downtown hotels, sitting in parks and eating in cheap restaurants, are old people in various degrees and sorts of isolation. Not all who are isolated feel lonely and not all who feel lonely are isolated. But even for the confirmed urban hermit, isolation may be involuntary. Or rather, the choices of whom to see and talk with are made within an increasingly narrow band of alternatives.

Isolation is not randomly distributed across the class hierarchy; there is more of it at the bottom. It is commonly said that old age is a leveler, that it affects the rich in the same way it affects the poor. It doesn't. The rich fare better in old age even as they fared better in youth. The poorer you are, the shorter your life expectancy, the poorer your health and health care, the lower your morale generally, the more likely you are to "feel" old regardless of your actual age, the less likely you are to join clubs or associations, the less active you are and the more isolated, even from children. Irving Rosow's study of 1,200 people over 62 living in Cleveland found that roughly 40 percent of the working class but only 16 percent of the middle class had fewer than four good friends. Another study of 6,000 white working-class men and women showed that of those over 65 with incomes under $3,000, a full third did not visit with or speak to a friend or neighbor during the preceding week.[1] The rock bottom poor are isolated, but not only they.

The isolation of old people is linked to other problems. The old are poor and poverty itself is a problem. The old are unemployed and unemployment, in this society, is itself a problem. The old lack community and the lack of community is itself a problem. There is some connection between these three elements. Removed from the economy, the old have been cast out of the social networks that revolve around work. Lacking work, they are pushed down the social ladder. Being poor, they have fewer social ties. Poverty reinforces isolation. To eliminate enforced isolation, we have to eliminate poverty, for the two go together. The social life of Merrill Court residents, who had modest but not desperately low incomes, is an exception to the general link between social class and isolation.

I do not mean to imply that the problem of old age would be solved if every old person were in a Merrill Court. A small part of it could be solved if every old person who wanted to try it was able to. But the basic problem far exceeds the limits of tinkering with housing arrangements. It is not enough to try to foster friendships among the old. Even to do that, it is not enough to set up Bingo tables in the lobbies of decrepit hotels or to hand out name cards to the sitters on park benches. This would simply put a better face on poverty, a cheerful face on old age as it now is, at not much social cost.

Merrill Court is not set in any island of ideal social conditions; it is essentially an adjustment to bad social conditions. As Chapter Two suggests, for the lives of old people to change fundamentally, those *conditions* must change. In the meantime, Merrill Court is a start. It is a good example of what can be done to reduce isolation. I do not know if similar communities would have emerged in larger apartment houses or housing tracts rather than in a small apartment house, with the married rather than the widowed, with rich rather than poor residents, with people having a little in common rather than a lot, with the very old person rather than the younger old person. Only trying will tell.

Merrill Court may be a forecast of what is to come.[2] A survey I conducted of 105 University of California students in 1968 [3] suggested that few parents of these students and few of the students themselves expect to be living with their families when they are old. Nearly seven out of ten (69 percent) reported that "under no circumstances" would they want their aged parents to live with them, and only 3 percent expected to be living with their own future children when they are old. A full 28 percent expected to be living with *other* old people, and an additional 12 percent expected to be "living alone or with other old people."

Future communities of old people may be more middle class and more oriented toward leisure. The old of the future will probably differ from Molly, and Ada, and Daisy, and Ruby, and Beatrice. The survey showed that less than 10 percent of the students expected to be working when they passed 65. A great many expected to be "enjoying life," by which they meant studying, meditating, practicing hobbies, playing at sports, and traveling.

But some things about future communities may be the same.

As I have suggested throughout this book, communal solidarity can renew the social contact the old have with life. For old roles that are gone, new ones are available. If the world watches them less for being old, they watch one another more. Lacking responsibilities to the young, the old take on responsibilities toward one another. Moreover, in a society that raises an eyebrow at those who do not "act their age," the subculture encourages the old to dance, to sing, to flirt, and to joke. They talk frankly about death in a way less common between the old and young. They show one another how to be, and trade solutions to problems they have not faced before.

Such an unexpected community may be part of a "second adolescence." If some people return to second childhood in extreme old age, then perhaps they first pass through a stage that has something in common with adolescence. Just as some never emerge from the "first" adolescence, so some of the residents of Merrill Court never emerged, before they died, from the second. Just as the first adolescence does not develop in all cultures or under all conditions, so, too, with the second.

Like adolescence, old age is the minority group almost everyone joins. But it is a forgotten minority group from which many old people dissociate themselves. A Community such as Merrill Court counters this disaffiliation. In the wake of the declining family, it fosters a "we" feeling, and a nascent "old age consciousness." In the long run, this may be the most important contribution an old age community makes.

NOTES

Chapter One

[1] It is an odd thing that, as the bibliography shows, female researchers are over-represented in the field of social gerontology. Although many men have worked in the field, women have contributed much more to it than to almost any other field outside of education and the family. Many old people, like children, need to be taken care of and this may have a traditional appeal to women. But it may also be that women can more readily identify with the old. In this society, old age is to youth as female is to male; both old people and females are de-valued relative to their opposites. Moreover, age devalues women, on both the economic and the sexual market, sooner than it does men. These facts may help explain why a disproportionate number of women social scientists study old people.

[2] Cumming and Henry, 1961, p. 233.

[3] Recently, a number of sociologists have become more concerned with precisely how the observer translates what he notices into his scientific framework. That is, by what taken-for-granted rules does the observer pick out what is relevant and what is not and how does he verify his interpretations? (Dreitzel, 1970.) It would take another and different book to answer these intriguing, difficult questions. In doing par-ticipant observation, I ran into two problems (at least). For one thing, I wondered if I identified with the "false consciousness" of my subjects. I may have been persuaded that age-segregation was a good thing be-cause I identified with the old people who thought so. However, I do not think my conclusions can be explained away that way. For another thing, I did not know how many of my thoughts to share with my research subjects. I did not want to share interpretations or opinions that might modify their behavior. This was a real concern. The prejudiced remarks some of them made about Negroes before I expressed an opinion dissolved into pious generalities afterward. Most of the residents were conservative Democrats who favored law and order, the police officer's right to shoot to kill, discipline in the schools, compulsory prayer, and a hard policy on "lazy people who live on welfare." Most were themselves welfare recipients.

[4] See Lowenthal and Boler, 1965, pp. 363–365; Hunter and Maurice, 1953, p. 47; Langford, 1962, pp. 6–7; Evans, 1966, pp. 147–148. Also see Gurin *et al.*, 1960, pp. 235–237 and Phillips, 1957, p. 215. For the two studies showing the opposite trend, see Townsend, 1957, p. 124 and Blau, 1957.

⁵ In fact, in Cumming and Henry's study, women were slightly *more* likely to "disengage"—a process that involves voluntary withdrawal from other people. (Cumming and Henry, 1961.)

⁶ This comes from the ———— Board of Trade, 1887. Also see Vaz, 1965. For a study of working-class people from a very similar environment, see Berger, 1960–1966.

Chapter Two

¹ Arendt, 1959, p. 5.

² One study showed that 37 percent of old people thought that the old in general were still useful, but 83 percent felt that *they* personally were still useful (Rosow, 1967).

³ Gorer, 1964, p. 87.

⁴ *Ibid.*, p. 131.

⁵ See Neugarten and Moore, 1968, p. 12.

⁶ This is not to say that age-stratification and strong kinship ties are inversely related under all conditions. See Eisenstadt, 1956.

⁷ See Riley and Foner, 1968, p. 170. Some commentators say that the three-generation family has declined with time (Tartler, 1963) although others say that it has not, since it was never very common. (Riley and Foner, 1968.)

⁸ See Beyer and Woods, 1963.

⁹ See Rosow, 1961, 1962, 1967. Also see Messer, 1966, for a careful study showing the greater sociability of old people in age-segregated settings as compared to those in age-integrated settings.

¹⁰ See Blau, 1961.

¹¹ Community Welfare Council of Schenectady County, 1957. Also see Aldridge, 1959.

¹² See Bultena and Woods, 1969.

¹³ There were 607 in public housing and 105 in the control group. Both groups were all white, mainly female, in their late 60's and in fairly good health. Half of each group was widowed and a third of each group was on welfare. The author controlled for race, sex, age, perceived health, source of income, and education. Fewer of those rejected for housing were on welfare and most were in good health. (Lipman, 1968, p. 92.)

¹⁴ See Cumming and Henry, 1961. Also, for a fuller treatment of disengagement theory, see A. Hochschild, "A Community of Grandmothers," (Ph.D. Dissertation, 1969, University of California, Berkeley.) One study showed that disengagement is linked not to old age *per se* but to the loss of roles linked to age. If old people keep their work,

their health, and their spouse, regardless of their age they do not disengage. (Tallmar and Kutner, 1969). All the residents of Merrill Court have lost their roles as parents, all but one no longer work, and a majority are widowed. Thus, they have suffered "role loss," but in spite of that they have not disengaged, much as others in age-separated contexts have not.

Chapter Three

[1] However, the apartments that were vacated through death were taken by people who had previously joined the community and were known to the original residents.

[2] Let us assume that the behaviorist does not include verbal datum as behavior. See Homans, 1950.

[3] Some characteristics of the age peer community are common to other working-class voluntary organizations, although they perform unique functions for older people. Other characteristics appear to be unique to an age-segregated setting (see Chapter Four).

[4] See Wolff, 1950, p. 361. As Simmel put it, ". . . the internal, ritual regimentation of secret societies reflects a measure of freedom and severance from society at large which entails the counter-norm of this very schematism, in order to restore the equilibrium of human nature."

[5] See Becker, 1960, p. 805.

[6] See Blauner, 1968, for an incisive analysis of how the social structure accommodates death. In Merrill Court, the formal role structure did not have to change to accommodate death.

[7] Clark and Anderson note that many of their older respondents liked to help those less fortunate (1967, p. 315).

[8] Most old people do not consider themselves as old. Kutner *et al.,* found that relative to most people their age, 65 percent felt younger, (1956, pp. 94, 98). Relative to their actual age, over 40 percent of those over 65 think of themselves as younger, while less than 20 percent think of themselves as older. (Batten, Barton, Durstine and Osborn, Inc., 1966). Only a minority (less than a third) of those 60 and over think that people they care most about think of them as old (Barron, 1961, pp. 106–107). Feeling old is also linked to low socioeconomic status (Kutner *et al.,* 1956, p. 94) and to loss of major roles—the retired, and widowed (Phillips, 1957, p. 216).

[9] As Memmi points out, "It is a fact that misery consoles misery. Is it surprising then that the racist takes a rest from his own misery by looking at the next man's? He even goes one step further, claiming that the next man is more miserable, unfortunate and perverse than he really is." (See Memmi, 1968, p. 202.) Also, Thorstein Veblen in *The*

Theory of the Leisure Class discusses the belief in luck, noting its importance to economic efficiency. (Veblen, 1953, p. 184.)

[10] These two bonds crosscut the distinction between primary and secondary relations since both bonds can be either. They may be useful in analyzing social change. A hundred years ago, most primary relations were confined to a circle of kin. Parent-child and sibling bonds were found within kinship circles. Today, the nuclear family probably absorbs fewer of all primary relationships. These relational models, held as constants, can enable us to compare the structural context of an individual's relationships at Time$_1$ with that at Time$_2$. Taking the relationship rather than the family as a unit of analysis, we can trace social change not by looking at institutions, but by looking at the component relationships that build them up or tear them down.

[11] See Alvin Gouldner's excellent article, "The Norm of Reciprocity" (1960). Gouldner distinguishes between reciprocity and complementarity. Only in some cases do complementarity and reciprocity overlap (p. 164). ". . . complementarity connotes that one's rights are another's obligations and vice versa. Reciprocity, however, connotes that each party has rights *and* duties" (p. 169). This is crucial because if we mesh complementarity with reciprocity, we wrongly assume that when two parties divide labor they get equal returns.

[12] See Freud, 1966, p. 205. Freud had little to say about social siblings in relation to rivalry, but he notes in his *Introductory Lectures* the potential for rivalry between biological siblings; "A small child does not necessarily love his brothers and sisters; often he obviously does not . . ." (1966, p. 204).

[13] Richman, 1957, p. 197.

[14] The institutionalized are generally older, more likely to be female, widowed, white, to not have living children, to live alone prior to institutionalization, to be poor and physically impaired, and to be put there by "mistake." Goldfarb found that only 89 percent of the patients over 64 in mental hospitals "should" be there. (Goldfarb, 1961, p. 253.)

Townsend's study of 530 new residents in British old age homes showed only 18 percent with close friends inside the institution. (Townsend, 1962, pp. 343, 347.)

[15] See Cumming and Henry, 1961, p. 65, to whom I am indebted for their application of Durkheim to age-grading theory.

[16] In modern society, there is a special premium on the sibling bond. As I see it there is a tension between two trends. On one hand, rapid social change calls for social flexibility. On the other hand, the declining death rate and the aging of the population means that more generations are alive at any given time in 1960 than was true in 1900. This reduces social flexibility, since the old (for whatever reasons) tend to be more committed to old ways of doing things and less open to new ones. Mannheim remarked in his essay, "The Question of Genera-

tions," that if birth and death were not natural facts, we would have to invent them. Birth and death, he notes, are forms of collective remembering and forgetting. I suggest that the functional equivalent to death *has* been devised in the sibling bond. The solidarity within generations and the divisions between them split society into layers of perspective and layers of experience, thus enhancing social flexibility by making the younger layer more independent of the older one. See Mannheim, 1952, and Ryder, 1965.

Chapter Four

[1] Other authors find this too. See Rose, 1962; Rose and Peterson, 1965; Blau, 1956; Messer, 1966; Breen, 1963, p. 383; and Bultena and Wood, 1969.

[2] Neugarten and Peterson have shown that age appropriate norms are held more strongly by older people than younger (1957). Possibly, then, it is the middle-aged children or the old people who impose constraints on themselves.

[3] See Erikson, 1959, p. 98.

[4] In Cumming and Henry's work, *Growing Old,* they found a tiny fraction of their sample admitted to ever thinking of death or dying (footnote, p. 93). Ironically, their sample of fairly inactive "disengaged" older people seem *more* reluctant to talk of death—the ultimate disengagement—than are the active residents of Merrill Court, whom one might suspect of denying death. Other studies show findings more like my own (Lieberman, 1966; Kogan and Shelton, 1962-b).

[5] Gorer's study *Grief Without Mourning* (1965), notes the absence of such occasions on which to express grief in modern society, and it may be that other old people do not have the opportunity to release their emotions as much as do the residents of Merrill Court. On the other hand, the opportunity afforded by this "old-fashioned way of dying" has another side. During the dinners for the families of the deceased, there is a general taboo on cheerful topics, and one is, in fact, "expected to mourn," even if at that time a person does not feel mournful. The shoe is on the other foot.

[6] Philip Slater writes: "The 'phantom limb' experiences of amputees are precisely the same as the hallucinations of the bereaved. Indeed, the use of the term, 'phantom' in the above phrase serves to remind us that the very idea of ghosts, which is practically universal, is an expression of this phenomenon. A majority of contemporary primitive societies, not to mention all of those which played a part in the development of our own civilization, hold the belief that the spirits of the dead hover around the living for a time, and are dispersed only at the conclusion of funerary rites or a prescribed mourning period, or upon

finally being told or magically compelled to depart. These ancestral shades are simply the 'phantom limbs' of the society, persisting until they have been decathected by their loved ones, i.e., until the mourning process has fulfilled its course as described by Freud. . . ." (Philip Slater, "Prolegomena To a Psychoanalytic Theory of Aging and Death." Also see Freud's essay, "Mourning and Melancholia," in Rickman, 1957.

[7] See Blauner, 1968.

[8] See Slater, 1963.

Chapter Five

[1] See Rose, 1962.

[2] Three-fourths of those over 65 have living children, and of those, eight-tenths see a child as often as once a week, and two-thirds see at least one child as often as every day or two (Stehouwer, 1965, p. 147). Stehouwer found that although living arrangements varied in Denmark, Great Britain, and the United States, frequency of interaction did not.

[3] See Bott, 1957 and Adams, 1969.

[4] Komarovsky, 1950, notes the same pattern. Townsend found that contacts were more frequent between old people and daughters, more frequent with youngest compared to oldest son or daughter (even when both are married), and more frequent in large families than in small ones (Townsend, 1957, pp. 38, 87–88, 200).

[5] Armstrong, 1959, p. 55.

[6] Clark and Anderson, 1969, p. 303 and Cumming and Henry, 1961, found the same thing. However, Messer found that older people in age-segregated settings are less likely (by about 20 percent) to see their relatives or children at least once a week than are older people in age-segregated settings (Messer, 1966, p. 57). I originally thought this would also be the case in Merrill Court.

[7] The slight tilt in reciprocity in the parent-child relation is reversed in the population at large. Streib's study of 1,300 retired and employed males aged 69 showed that parents help their children just a bit more than children help them (1958, p. 57; also see Shanas, 1966). But helping children is slightly more common in the middle class and in urban areas than it is in the lower class and rural areas (Riley and Foner, 1968, p. 552). Regardless of class, females are more likely to receive help than males (Shanas, 1966). The fact that Merrill Court is composed of lower-class rural-bred women may account for the different balance of give and take between the generations. (See Bond, 1960; Robins, 1962; Streib and Thompson, 1960).

[8] See Kreps, 1965.

[9] The *Random House Dictionary* gives several definitions of "identification." Sociologically it means "an acceptance as one's own of the values and interests of a social group." Psychologically it means, "a process by which a person ascribes to himself the qualities or characteristics of another person." Psychoanalytically it means, "the transference or reaction to one person with the feelings or responses relevant to another." Generally, it means the "perception of another as an extension of oneself." I use the term in the general sense.

[10] Anna Freud, 1966, p. 125. Reprinted with permission of International Universities Press.

[11] *Ibid.*, p. 126.

[12] It is also possible that altruistic surrender is linked to what Gutmann calls "passive masterly style." According to Gutmann, there are three main types of ego mastery—active mastery (the individual strives for autonomy, competence and control), passive mastery (he adapts, complies and identifies with those who control), and magical mastery (the boundaries between self and other are nullified through real or symbolic acts of incorporation). As the individual ages, he moves along a continuum from active to passive to magical mastery. (See Gutmann, 1967, 1968). Bernice Neugarten has noted that for women the trend is reversed; passive young women become more autonomous, assertive old women (1968). If the Merrill Court grandmothers are generally more assertive than they once were (and we do not know this for sure) they seem to be more passive in relation to their children, and more active in relation to their peers. If women become less passive as they grow older, it is all the more remarkable that we should find evidence of passive identification in older women. It is even more probable that we should find it in young women whose propensity for active mastery is submerged by the social equation of femininity with passivity.

[13] See Rogoff, 1953.

[14] The differences between the grandmothers and their daughters and granddaughters was not only a result of their different stages in the life cycle but also of their different places in history and the social-class structure. However, the differences in social place and history, as Erik Erikson has pointed out, intermesh with the life cycle.

According to Erikson's theory, every individual in every culture passes through eight stages of socio-emotional development; the childhood stages (trust vs. distrust, autonomy vs. shame, industry vs. inferiority), the adolescent stage (identity vs. role diffusion), the adult stage (intimacy vs. isolation, and generativity vs. despair), and finally the stage of old age (integrity vs. despair). To each stage is attached a crisis and how one faces each crisis, and indeed its very meaning, varies with the time, social context, and social class of the people involved. Erikson's description of what occurs during these stages does not fit working-class people such as the residents of Merrill Court or their daughters. His theory rests on clinical data on mainly upper-middle-class patients. The grandmothers and their daughters have probably never seen a psychiatrist's couch, and this is a loss to psychiatric theory as well as to the grandmothers and people like them. The grandmothers were young children of small farmers at a time when three-fourths of Americans lived in rural areas. The first stages of life (trust vs. distrust, autonomy vs. shame and doubt, industry vs. inferiority) took place in a context that rewarded industry and autonomy and made miniature adults of the little "child-mothers" who watched over their numerous siblings while working around the kitchen and barnyard. The stress was on industry that corresponded to a clear social need. They look back with satisfaction on this phase of life and compare it favorably to the childhoods of their more affluent grandchildren who more typically work at play than play at work. In adolescence there was little to suggest an "identity crisis." Their lower-class life style and the times provided no age-segregated institutions, no notable subculture of age peers attached to the school that might foster a "psycho-social moratorium on adulthood." Far from holding off on adulthood, they entered it as teenage brides and, often, mothers (most were married by age 17). Only a few recalled a "turning point" in adolescence that they linked to "being reborn" at a local Baptist revival meeting. Again, in the next stage, intimacy vs. isolation, the grandmothers did not experience the typical middle-class intimacy with their husbands. They often spoke of their husbands as providers but seldom as companions. They were more likely to be close to a sister or sister-in-law or female neighbor of the same age. And the final stage, integrity vs. despair, may also turn out to differ by generation and social class. Thus, the contexts of their life cycle are different from those of middle-class or younger people, and the crises themselves seem to have yielded to their socio-historical settings.

[25] Knupfer 1953, p. 259.

Chapter Six

[1] Grotjahn, 1964.
[2] See K. Erikson, 1966 and Hoggart, 1961, pp. 249–282.
[3] See Thompson, 1963.
[4] See Boggs, 1965.
[5] Knox Brown, 1963, pp. 68–69.
[6] See Burgess, 1960-b.

Epilogue

[1] See Rosow, 1967, p. 59; Rosenberg, 1967, pp. 13–20; Hunter and Maurice, 1953, p. 44; and Kutner *et al.*, 1956, p. 59. They all find the same relationship between social class and friendship in old age.

[2] The Department of Health, Education and Welfare has already provided over a million dollars in grants for experiments in "cooperative or communal living for old people." Experiments have started in Philadelphia, Kansas City, Honolulu, Syracuse, New York City and Washington, D.C. In Kansas City, for example, the Institute for Community Studies is establishing "affiliated houses," or arrangements for unrelated older people to share household expenses, duties, and responsibilities.

[3] The survey was carried out in connection with my dissertation in the Spring of 1968. Questionnaires were distributed to an Introductory Sociology and a Social Problems class. Forty-two percent were males, 58 percent females. Forty-seven percent were between 18 and 20 years old, and only 7 percent were over age 26. Only 9 percent expected to be working once they were past 65. The study included a question "What do you want your life to be like when you are past 65?" Only 8.6 percent expected to be working and 2 percent to be active in politics. The single most common response (42 percent) was "enjoying life" by which 19 percent meant studying and meditation and by which the rest meant traveling, practicing hobbies and enjoying sports.

REFERENCES

Adams, Bert (1969)
Kinship in an Urban Setting. Chicago: Markham Publishing Co.

Albee, Edward (1961)
The American Dream. New York: Signet Books, 1961.

Albrecht, Ruth (1951)
"The Social Roles of Old People," *Journal of Gerontology,* Vol. 6, No. 2, pp. 138–145.

—— (1953)
"Relationships of Older People With Their Own Parents," *Marriage and Family Living,* Vol. 15, No. 4, pp. 296–298.

———— (1954)
"The Parental Responsibilities of Grandparents," *Marriage and Family Living,* Vol. 16, No. 3, pp. 201–204.

———— (1962)
Aging in a Changing Society. Gainesville, Florida: University of Florida Press.

Aldridge, C. Knight (1959)
"Informal Social Relationships in a Retirement Community," *Marriage and Family Living,* Vol. 21, No. 1, pp. 70–72.

Alleger, Daniel E. (ed.) (1964)
Social Change and Aging in the 20th Century. Report of the 13th Annual Southern Conference on Gerontology. Gainesville, Florida: University of Florida Press.

Alexander, Irving E., and Arthur M. Adlerstein (1959)
"Death and Religion," in Herman Feifel, (ed.) *The Meaning of Death.* New York: McGraw-Hill Book Company, pp. 271–283.

Allen, Frederick Lewis (1965)
The Big Change: America Transforms Itself: 1900–1950. New York: Bantam Books.

Altrocchi, John, and Carl Eisdorfer (1962)
"Comparison of Attitudes Toward Old Age, Mental Illness and Other Concepts," in Clark Tibbitts and Wilma Donahue (eds.) *Social and Psychological Aspects of Aging.* New York: Columbia University Press, pp. 860–865.

Anderson, John E. (1964)
"Psychological Research on Changes and Transformations During Development and Aging," in *The Relation of Development and Aging,* James Birren (ed.). Springfield, Illinois: Thomas Publishing Co.

Archibald, Katherine (1947)
Wartime Shipyard: A Study in Social Disunity. Berkeley and Los Angeles: University of California Press.

Arendt, Hannah (1959)
The Human Condition. Garden City, New York: Doubleday Anchor Books.

Aries, Philippe (1967)
"La Mort Inversée: Le Changement des Attitudes Devant la Mort

dans les Sociétiés Occidentales," *Archives Europeénnes de Sociologie,* Tome VIII, No. 2, pp. 169–195.

Armstrong, Charlotte (1959)
The Seventeen Widows of San Souci. New York: Coward McCann Inc.

Arth, J. J. (1961)
"American Culture and the Phenomenon of Friendship in the Aged," *The Gerontologist,* Vol. 1, No. 2, pp. 168–170. Also Tibbitts and Donahue (eds.), *Social and Psychological Aspects of Aging, ibid.,* pp. 529–534.

Babchuk, Nicholas, and Alan Booth (1969)
"Voluntary Association Membership: A Longitudinal Analysis," *American Sociological Review,* Vol. 34, No. 1, pp. 31–45.

Back, Kurt, and Carleton Guptill (1966)
"Retirement and Self Ratings," in Ida Simpson and John C. McKinney (eds.), *Social Aspects of Aging,* Durham: Duke University Press, Chapter 7.

————, and Kenneth Gergen (1966)
"Cognitive and Motivational Factors in Aging and Disengagement," in Simpson and McKinney (eds.), *Social Aspects of Aging, ibid.,* Chapter 18.

Barker, Michael B. (1966)
California Retirement Communities. The Center for Real Estate and Urban Economics. Institute of Urban and Regional Development. University of California, Berkeley.

Barron, Milton (1953)
"Minority Group Characteristics of the Aged in American Society," *Journal of Gerontology,* Vol. 8, No. 4, pp. 477–482.

———— (1961)
The Aging American: An Introduction to Social Gerontology and Geriatrics. New York: Thomas Y. Crowell Co.

Bart, Pauline (1972)
Portnoy's Mother's Complaint. New York: Atherton Press.

Barton, Allen H., and Paul F. Lazarsfeld (1955)
"Some Functions of Qualitative Analysis in Social Research." Bobbs Merrill Reprint Series in the Social Sciences, S-336.

Bateson, Gregory (1950)
"Cultural Ideas About Aging," in *Research on Aging: Proceedings of a Conference Held on August 7–10,* University of California, Berkeley, Harold Jones (ed.). Pacific Coast Committee on Old Age Research, Social Science Research Council.

Batten, Barton, Durstine and Osborn Inc. (1966)
Report: An Investigation of People's Feelings on Age. .BBD&O Research Memorandum (unpublished).

Becker, Howard (1960)
"Normative Reactions to Normlessness," *American Sociological Review,* Vol. 25, No. 6, pp. 803–809.

Benedict, Ruth (1938)
"Continuities and Discontinuities in Cultural Conditioning," *Psychiatry,* Vol. 1, pp. 161–167. Bobbs Merrill Reprint Series in the Social Sciences, S-18.

Bennett, Ruth, and Lucille Nahemow (1965)
"Institutional Totality and Criteria of Social Adjustment in Residences for the Aged," *Journal of Social Issues,* Vol. 21, No. 4, pp. 44–75.

Berger, Bennett (1960-a)
"How Long Is a Generation?" *British Journal of Sociology,* Vol. 11, pp. 19–23.

———— (1960-b)
Working Class Suburb. Berkeley: University of California Press.

Beyer, Glenn (1962)
"Living Arrangements, Attitudes and Preferences of Older People," in Tibbitts and Donahue (eds.), *Social and Psychological Aspects of Aging, ibid.,* pp. 348–369.

————, and Margaret E. Woods (1963)
Living and Activity Patterns of the Aged. Research Report, No. 6. Ithaca, New York: Center for Housing and Environmental Studies, Cornell University.

Bianchi, Marcello Cosa, and Giancario Trentini (1962)
"A Further Contribution to the Study of Adjustment in Old Age," in Tibbitts and Donahue (eds.), *Social and Psychological Aspects of Aging, ibid.,* pp. 623–627.

Bibring, Edward (1968)
"The Mechanisms of Depression," In Phyllis Greenacre (ed.) *Affective Disorders,* New York: International Universities Press.

Birren, James E. (1959)
Handbook of Aging and the Individual. Chicago: University of Chicago Press.

—— *et. al.* (eds.) (1963)
Human Aging. Bethesda, Maryland: U.S. Public Health Service, Publication No. 986.

Blau, Zena Smith (1956)
"Changes in Status and Age Identification," *American Sociological Review,* Vol. 21, No. 1, pp. 198–203.

—— (1957)
"Old Age: A Study in Change in Status," Ph.D. Dissertation, Columbia University.

—— (1961)
"Structural Constraints on Friendship in Old Age," *American Sociological Review,* Vol. 26, No. 3, pp. 429–439.

Blauner, Robert (1968)
"Death and the Social Structure," in *Sociology and Everyday Life,* Marcello Truzzi (ed.). Englewood Cliffs, New Jersey: Prentice Hall, Inc.

Bloom, Kenneth L. (1961)
"Age and the Self Concept," *American Journal of Psychiatry,* Vol. 118, pp. 534–538.

Boggs, Sarah (1965)
"Urban Crime Patterns," *American Sociological Review,* Vol. 30, No. 6, pp. 899–908.

Bogue, Donald J. (1959)
The Population of the United States. Glencoe, Illinois: The Free Press.

Bond, Floyd, Ray Barber, John Vieg, Louis Perry, Alvin Scaff, and Luther Lee (1954).
Our Needy Aged: A California Study of a National Problem. New York: Holt, Rinehart and Winston.

—— *et al.* (1960)
"Financial Support of Parents: Some Attitudes and Opinions from

California," in Clark Tibbitts (ed.), *Handbook of Social Geron-tology: Societal Aspects of Aging.* Chicago: University of Chicago Press.

Bortner, R. (1962)
"Test Differences Attributable to Age, Selection, Processes and Institutional Effects," *Journal of Gerontology,* Vol. 17, No. 1, pp. 58–60.

Bott, Elizabeth (1957)
Family and Social Network. London: Tavistock Publications Ltd.

Breen, Leonard (1963)
"Retirement-Norms, Behavior and Functional Aspects of Norma-tive Behavior," in R. H. Williams, C. Tibbitts and Wilma Donahue (eds.) *Process of Aging,* Vol. 2, Chapter 47. New York: Atherton Press.

Brennan, Michael J., Philip Taft and Mark B. Schupack (1967) *The Economics of Age.* New York: W. W. Norton and Co.

Brim, O. B. (1968)
"Adult Socialization," in John Clausen (ed.), *Socialization and So-ciety.* Social Science Research Council. Boston: Little, Brown and Co., Chapter 5, pp. 182–226.

Brissette, Gerard, G. (1967)
The Significance of Life-Goals in Aging Adjustment—A Pilot Study. Sacramento, California: California Mental Health Research Mono-graph No. 9, 88 pp.

Bronson, W. E., E. S. Katten, and N. Livson (1959)
"Patterns of Authority and Affection in Two Generations," *Journal of Abnormal and Social Psychology,* Vol. 58, No. 2, pp. 143–152.

Bourque, L. B., and K. Back (1969)
"The Middle Years Seen Through the Life Graph," *Sociological Symposium,* No. 3, pp. 19–30.

Brown, R. G. (1960)
"Family Structure and Social Isolation of Older Persons," *Journal of Gerontology,* Vol. 15, No. 2, pp. 170–174.

Brown, Knox (1963)
Trust Officer, Pittsburgh National Bank, in Seminar on Protective Services for Older People, Arden House, New York, March 10–15.

Buhler, Charlotte (1935)
"The Curve of Life as Studied in Biographies," *Journal of Applied Psychology*, Vol. 19, pp. 405–409.

——— (1951)
"Maturation and Motivation," *Personality*, Vol. 1, pp. 184–211.

——— (1959)
"Theoretical Observations About Life's Basic Tendencies," *Journal of Psychotherapy*, Vol. 13, pp. 561–581.

——— (1961)
"Meaningful Living in the Mature Years," in R. W. Kleemeier (ed.), *Aging and Leisure*, New York: Oxford University Press, pp. 345–387.

——— (1961)
"Old Age and Fulfillment of Life With Considerations of the Use of Time in Old Age," *Vita Humana*, Vol. 4, pp. 129–133.

——— (1962)
"Genetic Aspects of the Self," *Annals of the New York Academy of Science*, Vol. 96, pp. 730–764.

Bultena, Gordon L., and Vivian Wood (1969)
"The American Retirement Community: Bane or Blessing?" *Journal of Gerontology*, Vol. 24, No. 2, pp. 209–217.

Burger, Ninki Hart (1968)
The Executive's Wife. New York: The Macmillan Co.

Burgess, Ernest (ed.) (1960-a)
Aging in Western Societies. Chicago: University of Chicago Press.

——— (1960-b)
"Family Structure and Relationships," in Ernest W. Burgess (ed.), *Aging in Western Societies*, Chicago: University of Chicago Press, pp. 271–298.

Burnight, Robert G., and Parker G. Marden (1967)
"Social Correlates of Weight in an Aging Population," *Milbank Memorial Fund Quarterly*, Vol. 45, No. 2, Part 1, pp. 75–92.

Butler, Robert N. (1963)
"The Life Review: An Interpretation of Reminiscence in the Aged," *Psychiatry*, Vol. 26, pp. 65–76.

Cain, Leonard (1964)
"Life Course and Social Structure," in R. E. L. Faris (ed.), *Hand-

book of Modern Sociology. Chicago: Rand McNally and Co., pp. 272–309.

Carp, Frances (ed.) (1966-a)
The Retirement Process. Report of a Conference, Gaithersburg, Maryland. U.S. Department of Health, Education and Welfare.

—— (1966-b)
A Future for the Aged: The Residents of Victoria Plaza. Austin, Texas: University of Texas Press.

—— (1967)
"Research Studies on the Aged," *Welfare in Review*, Vol. 5, No. 5, pp. 14–19. National Institute of Child Health and Human Development.

Cather, Willa (1956)
"Neighbour Rosicky," in *Five Stories*. New York: Vintage Books.

Cavan, Ruth, *et al.* (1949)
Personal Adjustment in Old Age. Chicago: Science Research Associates, Inc.

—— (1965)
"Family Tensions Between the Old and the Middle Aged," in Clyde Vedder (ed.), *The Problems of the Middle Aged*, Springfield, Illinois: Thomas Publishing Co., pp. 12–91.

Clark, Margaret, and Barbara Gallatin Anderson (1967)
Culture and Aging. Springfield, Illinois: Thomas Publishing Co.

—— (1968)
"The Anthropology of Aging: A New Area for Studies of Culture and Personality," in Bernice Neugarten (ed.) *Middle Age and Aging*, Chicago: University of Chicago Press, pp. 433–443.

Clausen, John (ed.), (1968)
Socialization and Society. Boston: Little, Brown and Co.

Cooper, William (1732)
Man Humbled By Being Comar'd to a Worm. Boston.

Cottrell, L. W. (1942)
"The Adjustment of the Individual to his Age and Sex Roles," *American Sociological Review*, Vol. 7, No. 5, pp. 617–620.

Cowgill, Donald (1958)
"Ecological Patterns of the Aged in American Cities," *Midwest Sociologist*, Vol. 20, No. 2, pp. 78–83.

Crittenden, John (1963)
"Aging and Political Participation," *Western Political Quarterly,* Vol. 16, No. 2, pp. 323–331.

Cumming, Elaine (1963)
"Further Thoughts on the Theory of Disengagement," *UNESCO International Social Science Journal,* Vol. 15, pp. 377–393.

Cumming, Elaine, Lois Dean, and David Newell (1958)
"What Is Morale? A Case History of a Validity Problem." *Human Organization,* Vol. 17, pp. 3–8.

———, and W. Henry (1961)
Growing Old: The Process of Disengagement. New York: Basic Books.

———, and I. McCaffrey (1961)
"Some Conditions Associated With Morale among the Aging," in P. Hoch and J. Zubin (eds.), *Psychopathology of Aging.* New York: Grune and Stratton.

———, and David Schneider (1966)
"Sibling Solidarity: A Property of American Kinship," in Bernard Farber (ed.), *Kinship and Family Organization.* New York: John Wiley & Sons, pp. 142–148.

Davis, Kingsley (1940)
"The Child and the Social Structure," *Journal of Educational Sociology,* Vol. 14, No. 4, pp. 217–229.

——— (1944)
"Adolescence and the Social Structure," in *The Annals of the American Academy of Political and Social Science,* Thorsten Selin (ed.), *Adolescence in Wartime,* Philadelphia, Vol. 236.

——— (1966)
Human Society. New York: The Macmillan Company.

Dean, Lois (1960)
"Aging and the Decline of Instrumentality," *Journal of Gerontology,* Vol. 15, No. 4, pp. 403–407.

——— (1962)
"Aging and Decline of Affect," *Journal of Gerontology,* Vol. 17, No. 4, pp. 440–446.

Desroches, H. F., and B. D. Kaiman (1964)
"Stability of Activity Participation in An Aged Population," *Journal of Gerontology*, Vol. 19, No. 2, pp. 211–214.

Dinkel, R. M. (1944)
"Attitudes of Children Toward Supporting Aged Parents," *American Sociological Review*, Vol. 9, No. 4, pp. 370–379.

Donahue, Wilma, Harold L. Orbach, and Otto Pollak (1960)
"Retirement: The Emerging Social Pattern," in Tibbitts (ed.), *Handbook of Social Gerontology, Ibid.* pp. 333–406.

Dovenmuehle, Robert H., and W. Edward McGough (1965)
"Aging, Culture and Affect: Predisposing Factors," *International Journal of Social Psychiatry*, Vol. 11, No. 2, pp. 138–146.

Downing, J. (1957)
"Factors Affecting the Selective Use of a Social Club for the Aged," *Journal of Gerontology*, Vol. 12, No. 1, pp. 81–85.

Drake, Joseph T. (1957)
"Some Factors Influencing Students' Attitudes Toward Older People," *Social Forces*, Vol. 35, No. 3, pp. 266–270.

——— (1958)
The Aged in American Society. New York: Ronald Press Co.

Dreitzel, Hans Peter (ed.) (1970)
Recent Sociology, No. 2. London: The Macmillan Company.

Duniman, Alexander P. (1960)
"Stratification Study of Television Programs," *Sociology and Social Research*, No. 4, Vol. 44, pp. 257–261.

Durkheim, Emile (1963)
Incest: The Nature and Origin of the Taboo, trans. by Edward Sagarin. New York: L. Stuart (originally published 1897).

——— (1949)
The Division of Labor in Society. Glencoe, Illinois: The Free Press.

Eisdorfer, C., and J. Altrocchi (1962)
"A Comparison of Attitudes Toward Old Age and Mental Illness," in Tibbitts and Donahue (eds.), *Social and Psychological Aspects of Aging, ibid.*, pp. 860–865.

Eisenstadt, S. N. (1956)
From Generation to Generation: Age Groups and Social Structure.
New York: The Free Press.

Emerson, Richard M. (1962)
"Power-Dependence Relations," *American Sociological Review.*
Vol. 27, No. 1, pp. 31–40.

Epstein, Lenore, and Janet H. Murray (1967)
The Aged Population of the United States: The 1963 Social Security Survey of the Aged. Washington, D.C.: Government Printing Office.

Erikson, Erik (1950)
Childhood and Society. New York: W. W. Norton and Co.

—— (1959)
"Identity and the Life Cycle," *Psychological Issues,* Monograph 1.
New York: International Universities Press, Inc.

Erikson, Kai (1966)
Wayward Puritans. New York: John Wiley & Sons.

Evans, Franklin B. (1966)
"When Death Us Do Part: The Problem and Adjustment of Middle Class American Widows" (unpublished).

Faris, Robert E. L. (1947)
"Interaction of Generations and Family Stability," *American Sociological Review,* Vol. 12, No. 2, pp. 159–164.

Feifel, Herman (1959)
The Meaning of Death. New York: McGraw-Hill Book Co.

Fenichel, Otto (1945)
The Psychoanalytic Theory of Neurosis. New York: W. W. Norton and Co.

Filer, Richard N., and Desmond D. O'Connell (1962)
"A Useful Contribution Climate for the Aging," *Journal of Gerontology,* Vol. 17, No. 1, pp. 51–57.

Frenkel-Brunswik, Else (1950)
"Wishes and Feelings of Duty in the Course of Human Life," in Harold Jones (ed.), *Research on Aging: Proceedings of a Conference Held on August 7–10,* University of California, Berkeley. Pacific Coast Commission on Old Age Research, Social Science Research Council.

Freud, Anna (1966)
The Ego and the Mechanisms of Defense (*The Writings of Anna Freud,* Vol. 11) New York: International Universities Press. (Originally published in German, 1936.)

Freud, Sigmund (1966)
The Complete Introductory Lectures on Psychoanalysis, trans. and ed. by James Strachey. New York: W. W. Norton and Co.

Friedenberg, Edgar (1963)
"The Role of the Adolescent in Adult Imagery and Feeling," in *The Vanishing Adolescent.* New York: Dell Publishing Co.

Friedmann, Eugene A. (1960)
"The Impact of Aging on the Social Structure," in Tibbitts (ed.), *Handbook of Social Gerontology, ibid.,* pp. 130–144.

Fromm, E. (1941)
Escape from Freedom. New York: Holt, Rinehart and Winston.

Fulton, Robert (ed.) (1965)
Death and Identity. New York: John Wiley & Sons.

Furnivall, J. S. (1956)
Colonial Policy and Practice: A Comparative Study of Burma and Indonesia. New York: New York University Press.

Furstenberg, Frank (June 1966)
"Industrialization and the American Family: A Backward Look," *American Sociological Review,* Vol. 31, No. 3, pp. 326–337.

Gans, Herbert (1962)
The Urban Villagers. New York: The Free Press.

Garber, Yonina Talmon (1962)
"Aging in Collective Settlements in Israel," in Tibbitts and Donahue (eds.), *Social and Psychological Aspects of Aging, ibid.,* pp. 426–441.

Garfinkel, Harold (1956)
"Conditions of Successful Degradation Ceremonies," *American Journal of Sociology,* Vol. 21, No. 5, pp. 420–424.

Garvin, Richard M., and Robert Burger (1968)
Where They Go to Die: The Tragedy of America's Aged. New York: Delacorte Press.

Genet, Jean (1961)
The Maids and Deathwatch. New York: Grove Press.

Gillespie, Michael (1967)
"The Effect of Residential Segregation on the Social Integration of the Aged" (mimeographed).

Given, K. (October 1969)
"But Would You Want One to Move Next Door?" *Car and Driver*, pp. 44–47.

Glaser, Barney (1967)
The Discovery of Grounded Theory: Strategies for Qualitative Research. Chicago: Aldine Publishing Co.

—— (1968)
Time for Dying. Chicago: Aldine Publishing Co.

Glaser, Barney, and Anselm Strauss (1964)
"Awareness Contexts and Social Interaction," *American Sociological Review*, Vol. 29, No. 5, pp. 669–678.

—— (1965)
Awareness of Dying. Chicago: Aldine Publishing Co.

Glick, Paul C. (1957)
American Families. New York: John Wiley & Sons; London: Chapman and Hall, Ltd.

Goffman, Erving (1959)
The Presentation of Self in Everyday Life. Garden City, New York: Doubleday Anchor Books.

—— (1961-a)
Asylums: Essays on the Social Situation of Mental Patients and Other Inmates. Garden City, New York: Doubleday.

—— (1961-b)
Encounters. New York: Bobbs Merrill Co.

—— (1963)
Behavior in Public Places. Glencoe, Ill: The Free Press of Glencoe.

—— (1964)
Stigma, Notes on the Management of Spoiled Identity. Englewood Cliffs, New Jersey: Prentice Hall.

Goldfarb, A. (1955)
"Psychotherapy of Aged Persons: One Aspect of the Psychodynamics of the Therapeutic Situation With Aged Patients," *Psychoanalytic Review*, Vol. 42, No. 2, pp. 180–187.

————— (1961)
"Current Trends in the Management of the Psychiatrically Ill Aged," in Paul H. Hoch and J. Zubin (eds.), *Psychopathology of Aging*. New York: Grune and Stratton, pp. 248–265.

Goldston, I. (1960)
"Our One-Generation Culture," *Public Aid*, III, Vol. 27, No. 10, pp. 10–12.

Goody, Jack (ed.) (1962)
The Developmental Cycle in Domestic Groups. Cambridge: Cambridge University Press.

Gordon, Margaret S. (1961)
"Work and Patterns of Retirement," in R. Kleemeier (ed.), *Aging and Leisure, ibid.,* pp. 15–54.

Gorer, Geoffrey (1964)
The American People. New York: W. W. Norton and Co. (rev. ed. 1948).

————— (1965)
Death, Grief, and Mourning. New York: Doubleday Anchor Books.

Gouldner, Alvin W. (1960)
"The Norm of Reciprocity," *American Sociological Review,* Vol. 25, No. 2, pp. 161–177.

Gravatt, Arthur E. (1953)
"Family Relations in Middle and Old Age: A Review," *Journal of Gerontology,* Vol. 8, No. 2, pp. 197–201.

Gray, H. (1947)
"Psychological Types and Changes With Age," *Journal of Clinical Psychology,* Vol. 3, pp. 273–277.

deGrazia, Sebastian (1961)
"The Uses of Time," in Kleemeier, *Aging and Leisure, ibid.,* pp. 113–153.

Greenacre, Phillis (ed.) (1968)
Affective Disorders. New York: International Universities Press.

Grotjahn, M. (1951)
"Some Analytic Observation About the Process of Growing Old," in Geza Roheim (ed.), *Psychoanalysis and the Social Sciences,* Vol. 3, New York: International Universities Press, pp. 301–312.

REFERENCES

———— (1964)
"Some Dynamics of Unconscious and Symbolic Communication in Present-Day Television," in W. Muensterberger and S. Axelrad (eds.), *The Psychoanalytic Study of Society*, Vol. III. New York: International Universities Press, pp. 356–372.

Gruen, Walter (1964)
"Adult Personality: An Empirical Study of Erikson's Theory of Ego Development," in Bernice Neugarten (ed.), *Personality in Middle and Later Life: Empirical Studies.* New York: Atherton Press.

Gurin, Gerlad, Joseph Veroff, and Sheila Felt (1960)
Americans View Their Mental Health: A Nationwide Interview Study. New York: Basic Books.

Gutmann, David, W. E. Henry, and B. L. Neugarten (1959)
"Personality Development in Middle-Aged Men." Presented at the Annual Meeting of the American Psychological Association, Cincinnati.

———— (1964)
"An Exploration of Ego Configurations in Middle and Later Life," in Neugarten, (ed.), *Personality in Middle and Later Life: Empirical Studies. Ibid.*

———— (1967)
"Ego Psychological and Developmental Approaches to the 'Retirement Crisis' in Men." NICHD Retirement Workshop, Washington, D.C., April 3–5 (Mimeographed)

———— (1968)
"The Country of Old Men: Cross-Cultural Studies in the Psychology of Later Life." Paper presented at Foundation's Fund for Research in Psychiatry, Conference on Adaptation to Change (mimeographed).

Hacker, Helen Mayer (1951)
"Women as a Minority Group," *Social Forces*, Vol. 30, No. 1, pp. 60–69. Bobbs Merrill Reprint Series in the Social Sciences, S-108.

Hausknecht, Murray (1962)
The Joiners: A Sociological Description of Voluntary Association Membership in the United States. New York: The Bedminster Press.

Havighurst, Robert J. (1954)
"Flexibility and the Social Roles of the Retired," *American Journal of Sociology,* Vol. 59, No. 4, pp. 309–311.

—— (1962)
"The Nature and Values of Meaningful Free Time Activity," in Tibbitts and Donahue (eds.), *Social and Psychological Aspects of Aging, ibid.,* pp. 899–904.

——, and Ruth Albrecht (1953)
Older People. New York: Longmans, Green and Co.

——, Bernice L. Neugarten and Sheldon S. Tobin (1963)
"Disengagement and Patterns of Aging." Unpublished manuscript read at the International Gerontological Research Seminar, Markaryd, Sweden, August.

——, and James Birren (1964)
"Introduction to the Study of Development and Aging in the Life Cycle," in James Birren (ed.), *Relations of Development and Aging.* Springfield, Illinois: Thomas Publishing Co.

Hawkinson, William P. (1965)
"Wish, Expectancy and Practice in the Interaction of Generations," in Arnold Rose and W. A. Peterson (eds.), *The Aging and Their Social World,* Philadelphia: F. A. Davis Co.

Henry, William E. (1963)
"The Theory of Intrinsic Disengagement." Unpublished manuscript read at the International Gerontological Research Seminar, Markaryd, Sweden, August.

—— (1965)
"Engagement and Disengagement: Toward a Theory of Adult Development," in Robert Kastenbaum (ed.), *Contributions to the Psycho-Biology of Aging.* New York: Springer Publishing Co., pp. 19–35.

Hill, Reuben (1965)
"Decision Making and the Family Life Cycle," in Ethel Shanas and Gordon Streib (eds.), *Social Structure and the Family: Generational Relations.* Englewood Cliffs, New Jersey: Prentice Hall, Chapter 6, pp. 113–141.

Hiller, E. T. (1947)
Social Relations and Structure: A Study in Principles of Sociology. New York, London: Harper and Brothers.

Hoar, Leonard (1680)
The Sting of Death and Death Unstung (sermon).

Hochschild, Arlie (1969)
"The Role of the Ambassador's Wife: An Exploratory Study," *Journal of Marriage and the Family,* Vol. 31, No. 1, pp. 73–87.

—— (1969)
"A Community of Grandmothers." Ph.D. Dissertation, Sociology Department, University of California, Berkeley.

Hoggart, Richard (1961)
The Uses of Literacy. Boston: Beacon Press.

Homans, George (1950)
The Human Group. New York: Harcourt, Brace and World.

Hoyt, G. C. (1954)
"The Life of the Retired in a Trailer Park," *American Journal of Sociology,* Vol. 59, No. 4, pp. 361–370.

Hunter, Woodrow W., and Helen Maurice (1953)
Older People Tell Their Story. Ann Arbor, Michigan: Institute for Human Adjustment, Division of Gerontology.

Hutchinson, Bertram (1954)
Old People in a Modern Australian Community. Cambridge: Cambridge University Press.

Hutschnecker, Arnold (1959)
"Personality Factors in Dying Patients," in Feifel, *ibid.*

Irish, Donald P. (1966)
"Sibling Interaction: A Neglected Aspect in Family Life Research," in Bernard Farber (ed.), *Kinship and Family Organization.* New York: John Wiley & Sons.

Jeffers, F. C., C. R. Nichols, and C. Eisdorfer (1962)
"Attitudes of Older Persons Toward Death: A Preliminary Study," in Tibbitts (ed.), *Social and Psychological Aspects of Aging, ibid.,* pp. 709–715.

Kagan, Jerome (1964)
"Change and Continuity in Development," Chapter 9, in Birren (ed.), *Relations of Development and Aging, Ibid.*

——, and H. A. Moss (1962)
Birth to Maturity. New York: John Wiley & Sons.

Kalish, R. A. (1965)
"The Aged and the Dying Process: the Inevitable Decisions," *Journal of Social Issues,* Vol. 21, No. 4, pp. 87–96.

Kaplan, Max (1960)
"The Uses of Leisure," in Tibbitts (ed.), *The Handbook of Social Gerontology, ibid.*

Karsten, Anitra (1961)
"Social Integration of the Aged in Finland," *Vita Humana,* Vol. 4, pp. 143–147.

Kastenbaum, Robert (1963)
"Cognitive and Personal Futurity in Later Life," *Journal of Individual Psychology,* Vol. 19, pp. 216–222.

——— (1965)
"Engrossment and Perspective in Later Life: A Developmental Field Approach," in Kastenbaum (ed.), *Contributions to the Psycho-Biology of Aging, ibid.*

———, and Nancy Durkee (1964)
"Young People View Old Age," in Kastenbaum, Robert (ed.), *New Thoughts on Old Age.* New York: Springer Publishing Co., pp. 237–249.

Kaufman, M. R. (1940)
"Old Age and Aging: The Psychoanalytic Point of View," *American Journal of Orthopsychiatry,* Vol. 10, pp. 73–79.

Kerckhoff, Alan (1965)
"Nuclear and Extended Family Relationships: a Normative and Behavioral Analysis," in Ethel Shanas and Gordon Streib (eds.), *Social Structure and the Family: Generational Relations.* Englewood Cliffs, New Jersey: Prentice Hall, Chapter 5, pp. 93–112.

——— (1966)
"Husband-Wife Expectations and Reactions to Retirement," in Simpson and McKinney (eds.), *Social Aspects of Aging, ibid.*

——— (1966)
"Norm Value Clusters and the 'Strain Toward Consistency' among Older Married Couples," in Simpson and McKinney (eds.), *Social Aspects of Aging, ibid.*

Kleemeier, R. W. (ed.) (1961)
Aging and Leisure. New York: Oxford University Press.

—— (1961)
"The Use and Meaning of Time in Special Settings: Retirement Communities, Homes for the Aged, Hospitals and Other Group Settings," in Kleemeier (ed), *Aging and Leisure, ibid.,* pp. 273–308.

Klein, Melanie (1955)
"On Identification," in *New Directions in Psychoanalysis.* London: Tavistock Publications.

—— (1957)
Envy and Gratitude: A Study of Unconscious Sources. New York: Basic Books.

Knupfer, Genevieve (1953)
"Portrait of an Underdog," in Reinhard Bendix and Seymour Martin Lipset (eds.), *Class, Status and Power.* Glencoe, Illinois: The Free Press of Glencoe, pp. 255–262.

Koch, Helen L. (1960)
"The Relation of Certain Formal Attributes of Siblings to Attitudes Held Toward Each Other and Toward Their Parents," *Monographs of the Society for Research in Child Development,* Serial no. 78, Vol. 25, No. 4, 41 pages.

Kogan, Nathan, and Michael A. Wallach (1961)
"Age Changes in Values and Attitudes," *Journal of Gerontology,* Vol. 16, No. 3, pp. 272–280.

Kogan, Nathan, and Florence C. Shelton (1962-a)
"Beliefs About 'Old People': A Comparative Study of Older and Younger Samples," *Journal of Genetic Psychology,* Vol. 100, pp. 93–111.

—— (1962-b)
"Images of 'Old People' and 'People in General' in an Older Sample," *Journal of Genetic Psychology,* Vol. 100, pp. 3–21.

Komarovsky, Mirra (1950)
"Functional Analysis of Sex Roles," *American Sociological Review,* Vol. 15, No. 4, pp. 508–516.

Kooy, Gerrit A. (1962)
"The Aged in the Rural Netherlands," in Tibbitts and Donahue (eds.), *Social and Psychological Aspects of Aging, ibid.,* pp. 501–509.

Kreps, Juanita (1965)
"The Economics of Intergenerational Relations," in Shanas and Streib (eds.), *Social Structure and the Family: Generational Relations, ibid.,* Chapter 12, pp. 267–289.

——— (ed.) (1966)
Technology, Manpower and Retirement Policy. Cleveland and New York: The World Publishing Co.

Kuhlen, R. G. (1948)
"Age Trends in Adjustment During the Adult Years as Reflected in Happiness Ratings." Paper read at meeting of the American Psychological Association, Boston.

——— (1964)
"Developmental Changes in Motivation During the Adult Years," in Birren (ed.), *Relations of Development and Aging, ibid.,* Chapter 13.

———, and G. H. Johnson (1952)
"Changes in Goals With Increasing Adult Age," *Journal of Consulting Psychology,* Vol. 16, pp. 1–4.

Kutner, B. *et al.* (1956)
Five Hundred Over Sixty. New York: Russell Sage Foundation.

Langford, Marilyn (1962)
Community Aspects of Housing for the Aged. Research Report, No. 5, Ithaca, New York: Center for Housing and Environmental Studies, Cornell University.

Lansing, J. B., and L. Kish (1957)
"Family Life Cycle as an Independent Variable," *American Sociological Review,* Vol. 22, No. 5, pp. 512–519.

Leyman, Harvey C. (1949)
"The Age of Eminent Leaders: Then and Now," *American Journal of Sociology,* Vol. 52, No. 1, pp. 342–356.

——— (1953)
Age and Achievement. Princeton: Princeton University Press.

——— (1962)
"More About Age and Achievement," *The Gerontologist,* Vol. 2, No. 3, pp. 141–148.

REFERENCES

Lieberman, Morton A. (1966)
"Observations on Death and Dying," *The Gerontologist*, Vol. 6, No. 2, pp. 70–72.

—— (1968)
"Psychological Correlates of Impending Death: Some Preliminary Observations," in Neugarten (ed.), *Middle Age and Aging, ibid.*, Chapter 56.

—— (1969)
"Institutionalization of the Aged: Effects on Behavior," *Journal of Gerontology*. Vol. 24, No. 3, pp. 330–340.

——, and Martin Lakin (1962)
"On Becoming an Institutionalized Aged Person," in *Processes of Aging, ibid.*, Chapter 22.

Linton, Ralph (1942)
"Age and Sex Categories," *American Sociological Review*, Vol. 7, No. 5, pp. 589–603.

Lipman, Aaron (1962)
"Role Conceptions of Couples in Retirement," in Tibbitts and Donahue (eds.), *Social and Psychological Aspects of Aging, ibid.*

—— (1968)
"Public Housing and Attitudinal Adjustment in Old Age, a Comparative Study," *Journal of Geriatric Psychiatry*, Vol. 2, No. 1, pp. 25–30.

Lipset, Seymour Martin (1950)
"An Aging Population in an Industrial Society: Sociological Aspects," in *Research on Aging. Proceedings of a Conference Held on August 7–10*, University of California, Berkeley, Harold Jones (ed.), Pacific Coast Committee on Old Age Research, Social Science Research Council.

Litwak, E. (1960)
"Occupational Mobility and Extended Family Cohesion," *American Sociological Review*, Vol. 25, No. 3, pp. 385–394.

—— (1965)
"Extended Kin Relations in an Industrial Democratic Society," in Shanas and Streib (eds.), *Social Structure and the Family: Generational Relations, ibid.*, Chapter 13, pp. 290–325.

Lowenthal, Marjorie Fiske (1964)
Lives in Distress: The Paths of the Elderly to the Psychiatric Ward.
New York: Basic Books.

————, and Deetje Boler (1965)
"Voluntary vs. Involuntary Social Withdrawal," *Journal of Gerontology*, Vol. 20, No. 3, pp. 363–371.

MacIver, R. M. (1962)
The Challenge of the Passing Years. New York: Trident Press, Simon and Schuster.

McKinney, John and Frank T. deVyver (eds.) (1966)
Aging and Social Policy. New York: Appleton-Century-Crofts.

Maddox, George L. (1963)
"Activity and Morale: A Longitudinal Study of Selected Elderly Subjects," *Social Forces*, Vol. 42, No. 2, pp. 195–204.

———— (1964)
"Disengagement Theory: A Critical Evaluation," *The Gerontologist*, Vol. 4, No. 2, pp. 80–83.

————, and Carl Eisdorfer (1962)
"Some Correlates of Activity and Morale Among the Elderly," *Social Forces*, Vol. 40, No. 3, pp. 254–260.

———— (1966)
"Sociological Perspectives in Gerontological Research." Presented at the 19th Annual Meeting of the Gerontological Society, New York City.

Mamovitc, Maurice (1966)
"Age Segregated Housing for the Middle-Class Aged." Proceedings, 7th International Congress of Gerontology, Vienna, pp. 551–553.

Mann, Thomas (1952)
Buddenbrooks. New York: Vintage Books.

Mannheim, Karl (1952)
"The Problem of Generations," in *Essays on the Sociology of Knowledge,* Chapter VII. New York: Oxford University Press.

Mannoni, O. (1956)
Prospero and Caliban: The Psychology of Colonization. London: Methuen and Co.

Marcuse, Herbert (1955)
Eros and Civilization. New York: Vintage Books.

Marris, Peter (1958)
Widows and Their Families. London: Routledge and Kegan Paul.

Martel, Martin U. (1968)
"Age-Sex Roles in American Magazine Fiction (1890–1955)," in Neugarten (ed.), *Middle Age and Aging, ibid.*

Martineau, Harriet (1837)
Society in America. New York: Saunders and Otley.

Mather, Cotton (1679)
"A Call from Heaven to the Present and Succeeding Generations." Boston, Sermon.

Mayer, Albert J., and Philip M. Hauser (1953)
"Class Differentials in Expectation of Life at Birth," in Reinhard Bendix and S. M. Lipset (eds.), *Class, Status and Power.* Glencoe, Illinois: The Free Press of Glencoe.

Mead, Margaret (1965)
And Keep Your Powder Dry. New York: William Morrow and Co.

Meier, Dorothy, and Bell, W. (1959)
"Anomie and Differential Access to the Achievement of Life Goals," *American Sociological Review,* Vol. 24, No. 2, pp. 189–202.

Memmi, Albert (1968)
Dominated Man. New York: Orion Press.

Mercer, Jane, and Edgar Butler (1967)
"Disengagement of the Aged Population and Response Differentials in Survey Research," *Social Forces,* Vol. 46, No. 1, pp. 89–96.

Merton, Robert (1957)
"Social Structure and Anomie," in Robert Merton, *Social Theory and Social Structure.* New York: The Free Press, pp. 131–160.

Messer, Mark (1966)
"The Effects of Age Groupings on Organizational and Normative Systems of the Elderly," Proceedings, Seventh International Congress of Gerontology, Vol. 6. Vienna: Wiener Medizinischen Akademie, pp. 253–258. Also Ph.D. Dissertation, Northwestern University.

Meyersohn, Rolf (1961)
"A Critical Examination of Commercial Entertainment," in Kleemeier (ed.), *Aging and Leisure, ibid.,* pp. 243–272.

Michelon, L. C. (1959)
"The New Leisure Class," *American Journal of Sociology,* Vol. 59, No. 4, pp. 371–378.

Milhoj, Poul (1962)
"Occupational Mobility in Aging," in Tibbitts and Donahue (eds.), *Social and Psychological Aspects of Aging, ibid.*

Miller, Stephen (1965)
"The Social Dilemma of the Aging Leisure Participant," in Rose (ed.), *The Aging and Their Social World, ibid.,* Chapter 5.

Mitford, Jessica (1963)
The American Way of Death. New York: Simon and Schuster.

Moore, Wilbert (1960)
"Changing Family Patterns, Why?" in Tibbitts (ed.), *Aging in Today's Society, ibid.,* pp. 175–181.

——— (1963)
Social Change. Englewood Cliffs, New Jersey: Prentice Hall.

——— (1963)
Man, Time and Society. New York: John Wiley & Sons.

——— (1966)
"Aging and the Social System," in John McKinney and Frank T. de Vyver (eds.), *Aging and Social Policy.* New York: Appleton-Century-Crofts, pp. 23–41.

Musgrove, Frank (1964)
Youth and the Social Order. London: Routledge and Kegan Paul.

Naville, Pierre (1962)
"The Role of Institutions in Fixing the Upper Limit of Productivity," in Tibbitts and Donahue (eds.), *Social and Psychological Aspects of Aging, ibid.,* pp. 64–75.

Neugarten, Bernice (1964-a)
Personality in Middle and Late Life: Empirical Studies. New York: Atherton Press.

——— (1964-b)
"A Developmental View of Adult Personality," in Birren (ed.), *Relations of Development and Aging, ibid.,* Chapter 12.

—— (1968)
"Adult Personality: Toward a Psychology of the Life Cycle," in Neugarten (ed.), *Middle Age and Aging, ibid.,* pp. 137–147.

——, and D. L. Gutmann (1958)
"Age-Sex Roles and Personality in Middle Age: A Thematic Apperception Study," *Psychological Monographs,* Vol. 72, No. 17, pp. 1–13.

——, and Joan W. Moore (1968)
"The Changing Age Status System," in Neugarten (ed.), *Middle Age and Aging, ibid.,* pp. 5–21.

——, and Warren Peterson (1957)
"A Study of the American Age-Grade System." Fourth Congress of the International Association of Gerontology, Vol. 3, Fiderza, Italy: Tito Mattioli., pp. 497–502.

Nimkoff, M. F. (1961)
"Changing Family Relationships of Older People in the United States During the Last 50 Years," *The Gerontologist,* Vol. 1, No. 2, pp. 92–97.

North, Cecil Clare (1926)
Social Differentiation. Chapel Hill: University of North Carolina Press.

Okada, Yuzura (1962)
"Changing Family Relations of Older People in Japan During the Last Fifty Years," in Tibbitts and Donahue (eds.), *Social and Psychological Aspects of Aging, ibid.*

Orbach, Harold (1962)
"Normative Aspects of Retirement," in Tibbitts and Donahue (eds.), *Social and Psychological Aspects of Aging, ibid.*

——, and Clark Tibbitts (ed.) (1963)
Aging and the Economy. Ann Arbor: The University of Michigan Press.

Parsons, Talcott (1954)
"Age and Sex in the Social Structure of the United States," in Parsons (ed.), *Essays in Sociological Theory.* New York: The Free Press, pp. 89–103.

────── (1963)
"Old Age as the Consummatory Phase," *The Gerontologist*, Vol. 3, No. 2, pp. 53–54.

Phillips, Bernard (1957)
"A Role Theory Approach to Adjustment in Old Age," *American Sociological Review*, Vol. 22, No. 2, p. 212–217.

Pinner, Frank, Paul Jacobs, and Philip Selznick (1959)
Old Age and Political Behavior: A Case Study. Berkeley and Los Angeles: University of California Press, Institute of Industrial Relations.

Powers, J. F. (1956)
The Presence of Grace. New York: Atheneum

Powles, William E. (1964)
"The Southern Appalachian Migrant: Country Boy Turned Blue-Collarite," in Arthur B. Shostak and William Gomberg (eds.), *Blue-Collar World*. Englewood Cliffs, New Jersey: Prentice Hall.

Prasad, S. B. (1964)
"The Retirement Postulate of the Disengagement Theory," *The Gerontologist*, Vol. 4, No. 1, pp. 20–23.

Rainwater, Lee, Richard P. Coleman, and Gerald Handel (1959)
Workingman's Wife. New York: Oceana Publications.

Reichard, Suzanne (1962)
"Personality and Adjustment to Aging," in Tibbitts and Donahue, (eds.), *Social and Psychological Aspects of Aging, ibid.*, pp. 666–669.

────── , Florine Livson, and Paul G. Peterson (1962)
Aging and Personality. New York: John Wiley & Sons.

Rheinstein, Max (1960)
"Duty of Children to Support Parents," in Burgess (ed.), *Aging in Western Societies, ibid.*, pp. 442–443.

────── (1965)
"Motivation of Intergenerational Behavior by Norms of Law," in Shanas and Streib (eds.), *Social Structure and the Family: Generational Relations, ibid.*, Chapter 11, pp. 241–266.

Richardson, Bessie Ellen (1933)
Old Age Among the Ancient Greeks. Baltimore: Johns Hopkins Press.

Rickman, James (ed.) (1957)
A General Selection from the Works of Sigmund Freud. Garden City, New York: Doubeday Anchor Books.

Riesman, David (1955)
"Some Clinical and Cultural Aspects of the Aging Process," in David Riesman (ed.), *Individualism Reconsidered.* Garden City, New York: Doubleday Anchor Books, pp. 164–173.

————, Nathan Glazer, and Reuel Denney (1961)
The Lonely Crowd. New Haven: Yale University Press (abridged edition).

Riley, John W. Jr. (1968)
"Attitudes Toward Death" (unpublished). See Matilda W. Riley and Anne Foner (eds.), *Aging and Society,* Vol. 1. New York: Russell Sage Foundation.

Riley, Matilda W., and Anne Foner (1968)
Aging and Society, Vol. 1. New York: Russell Sage Foundation.

Robins, Arthur (1962)
"Family Relations of the Aging in Three Generation Households," in Tibbitts and Donahue (eds.), *Social and Psychological Aspects of Aging, ibid.,* pp. 464–473.

Rogoff, Natalie (1953)
"Recent Trends in Urban Occupational Mobility," in Bendix and Lipset (eds.), *Class, Status and Power, ibid.,* pp. 442–453.

Rose, Arnold M. (1962)
"The Subculture of the Aging: A Topic for Sociological Research," *The Gerontologist,* Vol. 2, No. 3, pp. 123–127.

———— (ed.) (1963)
Aging in Minnesota. Minneapolis: University of Minnesota Press.

————, and W. A. Peterson (eds.) (1965)
The Aging and Their Social World. Philadelphia: F. A. Davis Co.

Rosen, Jacqueline, and Neugarten, Bernice (1960)
"Ego Functions in the Middle and Later Years: A Thematic Apperception Study of Normal Adults," in Neugarten, (ed.), *Personality in Middle and Late Life: Empirical Studies, ibid.,* pp. 90–101.

Rosenberg, George S. (1967)
Poverty, Aging and Social Isolation. Washington, D.C.: Bureau of Social Science Research.

Rosenfelt, Rosalie H. (1965)
"The Elderly Mystique," *Journal of Social Issues,* Vol. 21, No. 4, pp. 37–43.

Rosow, Irving (1961)
"Retirement Housing and Social Integration," *The Gerontologist,* Vol. 1, No. 2, pp. 85–91.

—— (1962)
"Old Age: One Moral Dilemma of Affluent Society," *The Gerontologist,* Vol. 2, No. 4, pp. 182–191.

—— (1963)
"Adjustment of the Normal Aged," in Williams, Tibbitts and *Donahue* (eds.), *Processes of Aging,* Vol. 2, Chapter 38. New York: Atherton Press.

—— (1965)
"Forms and Functions of Adult Socialization," *Social Forces,* Vol. 44, No. 1, pp. 35–45.

—— (1967)
Social Integration of the Aged. New York: The Free Press.

—— (1973)
"Socialization to Old Age," in press. National Institute of Child Health and Human Development. Bethesda, Maryland.

—— (1969)
"Retirement Leisure and Social Status." Durham: Duke University Center for the Study of Aging and Human Development.

Ruitenbeek, Hendrik (1969)
Death: Interpretations. New York: Dell Publishing Co.

Ryder, Norman (1965)
"The Cohort in the Study of Social Change," *American Sociological Review,* Vol. 30, No. 6, pp. 843–861.

Schatzman, L., and Strauss, Anselm (1955)
"Social Class and Modes of Communication," *American Journal of Sociology,* Vol. 60, No. 4, pp. 239–338.

Schorr, Alvin L. (1960)
Filial Responsibility in a Modern American Family. Washington, D.C.: Social Security Administration. U.S. Dept. of Health, Education and Welfare.

—— (1962)
"Filial Responsibility and the Aging, or Beyond Pluck and Luck," *Social Security Bulletin,* Vol. 25, pp. 4–9.

Schramm, Wilbur, and Ruth T. Storey (1961)
Little House: A Study of Senior Citizens. Stanford, California: Institute for Communication Research, Stanford University.

Senior Californian
Quarterly Publication of the California Commission on Aging, Sacramento, California, Vol. 1, No. 2.

Shanas, Ethel (1962)
The Health of Older People: A Social Survey. Cambridge: Harvard University Press.

—— (1962)
"Living Arrangements of Older People in the United States," in Tibbitts and Donahue (eds.), *Social and Psychological Aspects of Aging, ibid.,* pp. 459–463.

—— (1966)
"Family Help Patterns and Social Class in Three Countries." Presented at the Meetings of the American Sociological Association, Miami.

——, and Gordon Streib (eds.) (1965)
Social Structure and the Family: Generational Relations. Englewood Cliffs, New Jersey: Prentice Hall.

—— et al. (1968)
Old People in Three Industrial Societies. New York: Atherton Press.

Sheldon, Henry D. (1960)
"The Changing Demographic Profile," in TibbitꞱ (ed.), *The Handbook of Social Gerontology: Societal Aspects of Aging, ibid.*

——, and Clark Tibbitts (1950)
The Older Population of the United States. New York: John Wiley & Sons, Inc.

Shock, Nathan W. (1960)
    Aging: Some Social and Biological Aspects. Washington, D.C.:
    American Association for the Advancement of Science.

—— (1963)
    A Classified Bibliography of Gerontology and Geriatrics. Stanford, California: Stanford University Press.

Shostak, Arthur B., and William Gomberg (1964)
    Blue Collar World. Englewood Cliffs, New Jersey: Prentice Hall.

Simmons, Leo (1945)
    The Role of the Aged in Primitive Societies. New Haven: Yale University Press.

—— (1960)
    "Aging in Preindustrial Societies," in Tibbitts (ed.), *The Handbook of Social Gerontology: Societal Aspects of Aging, ibid.,* Chapter 3.

Simon and Garfunkel
    "Bookends" Song 6, "Old Friends."

Simpson, Ida Harper, and John C. McKinney (eds.) (1966)
    Social Aspects of Aging. Durham: Duke University Press.

Slater, Philip (1963)
    "Cultural Attitudes Toward the Aged," *Geriatrics,* April, pp. 308–314.

—— (date unstated)
    "Prologomena to a Psychoanalytic Theory of Aging and Death" (mimeographed).

——, and H. A. Scarr (1964)
    "Personality in Old Age," *Genetic Psychology Monographs,* Vol. 70, pp. 229–269.

Smith, Joel (1966)
    "Group Status of the Aged," in Simpson and McKinney (eds.), *Social Aspects of Aging, ibid.*

—— (1966)
    "The Narrowing Social World of the Aged," in Simpson and McKinney (eds.), *Social Aspects of Aging,* pp. 226–242.

—— and Herman Turk (1966)
    "Considerations Bearing on a Study of the Role of the Aged in

Community Integration," in Simpson and McKinney (eds.) *Social Aspects of Aging, ibid.*

Sommer, Robert, and Hugo Ross (1958)
"Social Interaction on a Geriatrics Ward," *International Journal of Social Psychiatry,* Vol. 4, No. 2, pp. 128–133.

Spark, Muriel (1960)
Memento Mori. New York: Meridian Books.

Spengler, Joseph J. (1966)
"Some Economic and Related Determinants Affecting the Older Worker's Occupational Role," in Simpson and McKinney (eds.), *Social Aspects of Aging, ibid.*

Statistical Abstracts of the United States (1968)
Department of Labor, Bureau of Labor Statistics.

Stehouwer, Jan (1965)
"Relations Between Generations and the Three-Generation Household in Denmark," in Shanas and Streib (eds.), *Social Structure and the Family: Generational Relations, ibid.,* pp. 142–162.

Steiner, Gary A. (1963)
The People Look at Television. New York: Alfred A. Knopf.

Streib, Gordon F. (1956)
"Morale of the Retired," *Social Problems,* Vol. 3, No. 4, pp. 270–276.

——— (1958)
"Family Patterns in Retirement," *Journal of Social Issues,* Vol. 24, No. 2, pp. 46–60.

——— (1965)
"Intergenerational Relations: Perspectives of the Two Generations on the Older Parent," *Journal of Marriage and the Family,* Vol. 27, No. 4, pp. 469–476.

———, and Wayne Thompson (1960)
"The Older Person in a Family Context," in Tibbitts (ed.), *The Handbook of Social Gerontology, ibid.,* Chapter 13.

Suchman, Edward A., Bernard S. Phillips, and Gordon F. Streib (1958)
"An Analysis of the Validity of Health Questionnaires," *Social Forces,* Vol. 36, No. 3, pp. 223–232.

Sudnow, David (1967)
Passing On: The Social Organization of Dying. Englewood Cliffs, New Jersey: Prentice Hall.

Sussman, M. B. (1954)
"Family Continuity: Selective Factors Which Affect Relationships Between Families at Generational Levels," *Marriage and Family Living,* Vol. 16, No. 3, pp. 112–120.

———— (1965)
"Relationships of Adult Children With Their Parents in the United States," in Shanas and Streib (eds.), *Social Structure and the Family: Generational Relations, ibid.,* Chapter 4, pp. 62–92.

Swenson, Wendell M. (1961)
"Attitudes Toward Death in an Aged Population," *Journal of Gerontology,* Vol. 16, No. 1, pp. 49–52.

Taietz, Philip, and Olaf Larson (1956)
"Social Participation and Old Age," *Rural Sociology,* Vol. 21, pp. 229–238.

Tallmar, Margot (1967)
"Social, Economic and Health Factors in Disengagement in the Aging." Ph.D. Dissertation, Yeshiva University, New York (June).

————, and Bernard Kutner (1969)
"Disengagement and the Stresses of Aging," *Journal of Gerontology,* Vol. 24, No. 1, pp. 70–75.

Tartler, Rudolf (1963)
"The Older Person in Family, Community and Society," Williams, Tibbitts and Donahue (eds.), *Processes of Aging, ibid.,* Vol. 11, New York: Atherton Press, Chapter 31.

Taeuber, Conrad, and Irene Taeuber (1958)
The Changing Population of the United States. New York: John Wiley & Sons.

Taves, Martin J., and Gary D. Hansen (1963)
"Seventeen Hundred Elderly Citizens," in Rose (ed.), *Aging in Minnesota, ibid.,* pp. 75–181.

Thomas, Hans (1961)
"Thematic Analyses of Aging," in Tibbitts and Donahue (eds.), *Social and Psychological Aspects of Aging, ibid.,* pp. 655–663.

Thompson, E. P. (1963)
The Making of the English Working Class. New York: Vintage Books.

Tibbitts, Clark (ed.) (1959)
Aging and Social Health in the United States and Europe. Report of an International Seminar held at Merano, Italy. July 9–13, 1957.

—— (ed.) (1960)
Handbook of Social Gerontology. Chicago: University of Chicago Press.

——, and Wilma Donahue (eds.) (1960)
Aging in Today's Society. Englewood Cliffs, New Jersey: Prentice-Hall.

—— and Wilma Donahue (eds.) (1962)
Social and Psychological Aspects of Aging. New York: Columbia University Press.

Tilly, Charles, and C. Harold Brown (1964)
"On Uprooting, Kinship and the Auspices of Migration." Joint Center for Urban Studies of Massachusetts Institute of Technology and Harvard University (unpublished draft).

Tobin, Sheldon S., and Bernice Neugarten (1961)
"Life Satisfaction and Social Interaction in the Aging," *Journal of Gerontology,* Vol. 16, No. 4, pp. 344–346.

deTocqueville, Alexis (1961)
Democracy in America, Vol. I and II, New York: Schocken Books.

Townsend, Peter (1957)
The Family Life of Old People. London: Routledge and Kegan Paul.

—— (1962)
"The Purpose of the Institution," in Tibbitts and Donahue (eds.), *Social and Psychological Aspects of Aging, ibid.*

Tuckman, Jacob, and Martha Lavell (1957)
"Self Classification as Old or Not Old," *Geriatrics,* Vol. 12, pp. 666–671.

—— and Irving Lorge (1953-a)
"When Aging Begins and Stereotypes about Aging," *Journal of Gerontology,* Vol. 8, No. 4, pp. 489–492.

————, and Irving Lorge (1953-b)
"Attitudes Toward Old People," *Journal of Social Psychology,* Vol. 37, May, pp. 249–260.

———— (1958)
"Attitude Toward Aging of Individuals with Experiences With the Aged," *Journal of Genetic Psychology,* Vol. 92, June, pp. 199–204.

United States Bureau of the Census (1960)
Census of Population, Vol. 1, Part 1.

U.S. Department of Labor, Bureau of Labor Standards (1965)
"Age Discrimination Prohibited Under State Laws." Fact Sheet No. 6-C.

United States Senate (1960)
Aging Americans: Their Views and Living Conditions. A Report by the Subcommittee on Problems of the Aged and Aging, Committee on Labor and Public Welfare.

Van Gennep, Arnold (1960)
Rites of Passage. Chicago: University of Chicago Press (originally published 1901).

Vaz, August Mark (1965)
The Portuguese in California. (Oakland: Irmandade do Vivino Espirito Santo I.D.E.S.) San Francisco: Filmer Brothers Press.

Veblen, Thorstein (1953)
The Theory of the Leisure Class. New York: Mentor Books.

Videbeck, Richard, and Alan B. Knox (1965)
"Alternative Participatory Responses to Aging," in Rose and Peterson (eds.), *Older People and Their Social World, ibid.,* pp. 37–48.

Von Hentig, H. (1946)
"The Social Function of the Grandmother," *Social Forces,* Vol. 24, No. 4, pp. 389–392.

Wallach, Michael A., and Leonard R. Green (1968)
"On Age and the Subjective Speed of Time," in Neurgarten (ed.), *Middle Age and Aging, ibid.,* pp. 481–485.

Wallach, Michael A., and Nathan Kogan (1961)
"Aspects of Judgment and Decision-making: Interrelationships and Changes with Age," *Behavioral Scientist,* Vol. 6, pp. 23–36.

REFERENCES

The Whisperers (a film)
film director, Bryan Forbes.

White, E. B. (July 1969)
"E. B. White at 70." Interview by Israel Shenker in the *International Herald Tribune.*

White, R. C. (1955)
"Social Class Differences in the Uses of Leisure," *American Journal of Sociology,* Vol. 61, No. 2, pp. 145–150.

Wilensky, Harold (1960)
"Work, Careers, and Social Integration," *International Social Science Journal,* Fall, Vol. 12, pp. 543–560.

—— (1961-a)
"Life Cycle, Work Situation and Participation in Formal Associations," in Kleemeier (ed.), *Aging and Leisure, ibid.,* pp. 214–242.

—— (1961-b)
"The Uneven Distribution of Leisure: the Impact of Economic Growth on Free Time," *Social Problems,* Summer, Vol. 9, pp. 32–56.

Williams, Richard H. (1968)
"Gemeinschaft and Gesellschaft in the Structure of American Society: Implications for Aging," in *Journal of Geriatric Psychiatry,* Fall, Vol. II, No. 1, pp. 6–18.

——, Clark Tibbitts, and Wilma Donahue (eds.) (1963)
Processes of Aging, 2 vols. New York: Atherton Press.

Williams, Robin M.
American Society: A Sociological Interpretation. New York: Alfred A. Knopf (2nd Ed.).

Willie, C. V. (1960)
"Age Status and Residential Stratification," *American Sociological Review,* Vol. 25, No. 2, pp. 260–264.

Wilner, Daniel M., and Rosabell P. Walkley (1966)
"Some Special Problems and Alternatives in Housing for Older Persons" in McKinney and deVyver, (eds.), *Aging and Social Policy. Ibid.*

Wolff, Kurt H. (trans.) (1950)
The Sociology of George Simmel. New York: The Free Press.

Yap, P. M. (1962)
"Aging in Underdeveloped Asian Countries," in Tibbitts and Donahue, (eds.), *Social and Psychological Aspects of Aging, ibid.,* pp. 442–458.

Youmans, E. Grant (1962)
"Leisure-Time Activities of Older Persons in Selected Rural and Urban Areas of Kentucky," *Progress Report 114,* Kentucky Agricultural Experiment Station, Lexington, Kentucky.

——— (1964)
"Personal Adjustment of Older Rural and Urban Persons," in Alleger (ed.), *Social Change and Aging in the 20th Century, ibid.,* pp. 78–85.

Young, Michael, and Peter Willmott (1957)
Family and Kinship in East London. Glencoe, Illinois: The Free Press.

Zawadski, Bohan, and Lazarsfeld, Paul F. (1935)
"The Psychological Consequences of Unemployment," *Journal of Social Psychology,* May, Vol. 6, pp. 224–251.

Zimand, Gertrude Folks (1944)
"The Changing Picture of Child Labor," *Annals of the American Academy of Political and Social Science,* Adolescents in War Time. Thorsten Sellin (ed.).

Zinberg, Norman E., and Irving Kaufman (eds.) (1963)
Normal Psychology of the Aging Process. New York: International Universities Press.

Zola, Irving Kenneth (1962)
"Feelings About Age Among Older People," *Journal of Gerontology,* Vol. 17, No. 1, pp. 65–68.

INDEX